ALONE

A HALEAKALA MEMOIR

RICK SCHEIDEMAN

ISBN: 978-1-66786-382-5

Dedication

For my daughters, Stefany, Heather, and Shannon; sons-in-law, Roy, Brent, and Andrew; and grandchildren, Cole, Anders, Benton, Noelle, Carter, Deveraux, Bobo, and Cambria.

The land knows you, even when you are lost.
—Robin Wall Kimmerer, *Braiding Sweetgrass*

In times when I cannot see one step ahead or behind me,
and I fear the unknown, you are with me.
—Psalm 23

TABLE OF CONTENTS

PREFACE

MOST people know Maui is one of the Hawaiian Islands situated between Oahu and the Big Island. But many may not be familiar with Haleakala, which occupies three-quarters of the island's landmass and is where the events in this account take place. Haleakala is a volcano that has erupted ten times in the past one thousand years, most recently between 1480 and 1600. It rises over ten thousand feet from sea level but extends another 19,680 feet (half of the cruising altitude of a commercial jet) making its total elevation 29,704 feet (about the height of Mt. Everest). Geologists believe that the eruptions that formed Haleakala began around a million years ago and estimate that it took some two hundred-thousand years to gain its present height and shape.

Hawaiians have their own traditional stories explaining the formation of the Hawaiian Islands that differ a bit from scientific theory. According to one myth, Pele, the goddess of fire, stomped her foot in various places, and wherever she stomped, an island came into being. There are several stories about how Maui's large volcano came by its name. One credits the demigod Maui, the island namesake, a mystical character who features prominently in many stories told throughout the southern Pacific Islands. It tells how La, the sun god, liked sleeping late, a habit that shortened his day significantly. Maui's mother, Hina, was upset by this situation because it made it hard for her to complete one of her most important tasks, making clothes from the bark of a tree that had to be dried before they could be pounded into cloth. Because of La's oversleeping, there wasn't enough heat to dry the bark that she needed, and Hina pestered her son to do something about this problem.

Early one morning, Maui hid on the summit of the volcano, waiting for La to come by as he did every morning after his long sleep to bring the sun up to the top. Maui fashioned a rope from coconut fiber and lassoed La, tying the other end to a Wiliwili tree. He refused to go until La promised to slow the movement of the sun in the arc of the sky so that Hina could make cloth. La agreed and as a result, the days got longer and hotter at the summit of the volcano, which became known as Haleakala, "The House of the Sun".

Haleakala's climate varies dramatically depending on the altitude and whether one is facing the windward side (rainy) or leeward side (dry). On any given day, the temperatures on Haleakala can vary from an average high of 80°F to a low of 30°F. Conditions change quickly on the upper reaches of the volcano with heavy clouds and rain replacing a warm sunshine. The northeast slopes of Haleakala become a rainforest that plunges into the Pacific. These factors play a role in the account you will read. When I'm at Haleakala, I often think of Mark Twain's description of his experience there in *Roughing It:*

> *"The chief pride of Maui is her dead volcano of Haleakala. We climbed a thousand feet up the side of this isolated colossus one afternoon; then camped, and the next day climbed the remaining nine thousand feet and anchored on the summit, where we built a fire and froze and roasted by turns, all night. With the first pallor of dawn, we got up and saw things that were new to us. Mounted on a commanding pinnacle, we watched Nature work her silent wonders. The sea was spread abroad on every hand, its tumbled surface seeming only wrinkled and dimpled in the distance*

A broad valley below appeared like an ample checker-board, its velvety green sugar plantations alternating with dun squares of barrenness and groves of trees diminished to mossy tufts

I have spoken of the outside view—but we had an inside one, too. That was the yawning dead crater, into which we now and then tumbled rocks, half as large as a barrel, from our perch, and saw them go careering down the almost perpendicular sides, bounding three hundred feet at a jump; kicking up cast-clouds wherever they struck; diminishing to our view as they sped farther into distance; growing invisible, finally, and only betraying their course by faint little puffs of dust; and coming to a halt at last in the bottom of the abyss.

Presently vagrant white clouds came drifting along, high over the sea and the valley; then they came in couples and groups; then in imposing squadrons; gradually joining their forces, they banked themselves solidly together, a thousand feet under us, and totally shut out land and ocean—not a vestige of anything was left in view but just a little of the rim of the crater, circling away from the pinnacle whereon we sat for a ghostly procession of wanderers from the filmy hosts without had drifted through a chasm in the crater wall and filed round and round . . . There was little conversation, for the impressive scene overawed speech. I felt like the Last Man, neglected of the judgment, and left pinnacled in mid-heaven, a forgotten relic of a vanished world.

It was the most sublime spectacle I have ever witnessed, and I think the memory of it will remain with me always."

—Mark Twain
Roughing It 1872

CHAPTER 1

Where am I?

THE raging inside my head feels like the jackhammer pounding of an earache. On and on, a metallic clanking does not stop. Only the modulation changes. It begins softly, then leaps up in volume, and I cannot turn it down. A strange voice chants inside the sound. My thoughts wobble in a fog of no sense; a vague question forms in my head, what is happening to me? Inside whispers of helplessness. I'm distant from myself. I'm not me. I don't know where I am. Only a bad dream? Again, I hear the voice, the voice inside the ceaseless clanking. This strange cacophony chants, "Je----sus Christ." "Je----sus Christ. Je----sus Christ," over and over again. It seems strange to even my foggy brain. My body feels numb, but fear blankets my emotions. Once again, my attention is dragged into these words, repeating "Je----sus Christ." I try to raise my hands to cover my ears to stop the voice. I can't. Something holds my wrists down. I can't reach my ears. I turn to look in the direction of the words. In the darkness, two tiny green lights blink off and on to the rhythm of the Jesus chant.

I'm desperate to escape from the metallic throb, the bright green blinking lights. I can't move. Fear grows with the constant sound. My legs don't move. Nothing moves except my hands that can't make it to my ears. Nothing in my mind sticks. A voice breaks in, low and gentle. I don't understand much. Words are vague.

"How are you feeling, Richard?"

I strain to mumble, "Can you hear it? A voice. Can you?"

"What do you hear?"

"It's a clanking sound. A voice. It keeps saying again and again 'Je—sus Christ. Je—sus Christ.' Can't you hear it?"

"You're okay, hon. You're safe. You're in the hospital now. We're going to take care of you. You'll be okay. Now just relax and try to sleep."

"Oh God, please help me. Make the voice stop. Please. Stop it. Stop the green lights. I can't move my legs. Help me!"

"It's okay, hon, the IV machine is old, so it makes noises. Yeah, it's kind of loud. I don't hear voices speaking, dear. You're in a safe place now. I'll be back soon, okay?"

It's not okay. I'm so damned scared. How much time passes I don't know, but later I awake to another voice, a different voice. A deep, quiet voice that I struggle to understand.

"How are you feeling, Mr. Scheideman?"

"Where am I?"

"You're in Maui Memorial Hospital. You've had an accident, but you are going to be okay. How do you feel?"

"I don't know. I'm so tired. There's something in my mouth, something big. I hurt. All over, I hurt. And the voice, do you hear it? Do you hear that? It won't stop. Can't you hear it? Make it stop."

"I understand. Try to sleep now. The voice will go away soon. The nurse will give you something to help you sleep."

I feel a cool hand on my forehead, then a prick on my arm.

When I wake, the loud voice is gone, but the green lights continue their blinking. I see a dim light across from my bed that seeps out behind something. A wall? The wall moves. Something leans against the wall because it bulges. The light darkens for a moment, and then lightens again with movement; maybe it's not a wall, but a curtain with someone leaning against it. I hear loud voices. Confusion overtakes me. I close my eyes and drift away. Several voices on top of each other turn into laughter. I startle awake with people talking. It hurts my ears.

Someone walks out from behind the curtain. I raise my head to look as they pass the foot of my bed. The voices come back, loud and laughing male voices. Someone crosses back and then behind the curtain with another person. More people move back and forth, passing by the foot of my bed. It sounds like they are having sex behind the curtain like they're having a party, a sex party. It goes on and on without stopping. It's very distressing. I try to put my hands over my ears, forgetting they're tied down. I want them to stop and be quiet.

A nurse comes by to check on me and I tell her about the sex party next to me. I ask her if she'd please tell them to stop what they are doing. I'm going to be sick. The nurse holds my head up and puts something under my chin. I throw up. When I'm through, she wipes my chin, touches my hand, and whispers, "Richard, the man next to you is very ill. His brother and friends are with him. They're speaking in whispers. Your room is quiet." She assures me twice more that there is no party or noise, but I don't believe her.

The low voice returns, "How's he doing?"

"He's stable, doctor, but still hallucinating."

"I don't know how he survived."

That's how I remember that night in the hospital, how I felt, and what was said. As I laid there, I hadn't a clue about how I got there, but thankfully I fell into a deep sleep.

CHAPTER 2

DREAMS

MY sleep was fitful. Sometimes when I woke, I had glimpses of scenes that I was beginning to remember. Freezing, soaked, starving, exhausted, completely disoriented, trying to find my way out. And then the ambulance and the hospital. That must have been last night. I remember the doctor and the nurse talking to me, and Kimberly, my wife, was there. I don't know what I said to her. I was sorry about something that happened, sorry that she worried. I was completely mixed up. Now my senses were beginning to return to me, and I tried to piece together what had happened the past few days. I couldn't. The effort proved too much, and I fell once more into a deep sleep.

I awoke soaked in sweat, the sounds of screams ringing in my ears. The nightmare remains in my mind. I'm standing above a body sprawled out on the ground, blood gushing from a vicious wound in her neck. I'm holding a long knife in my left hand. Strong lights illuminate the scene. It's not police floodlights but stage lighting. We are, in fact, on stage performing a scene we'd performed many times before. There's background music coming from speakers and mist created by a fog machine. At first, nothing seems amiss, but then an uneasy feeling comes over me. Something's wrong. I realize the knife in my hand is not a prop, and the blood is real. The actress below me is dead. I killed her. It's only a moment before the other cast members, crew, and audience realize what has happened and where the screams came from that woke me.

It certainly wasn't my first nightmare involving a stage calamity, but, of course, never like this one, definitely not true, and totally horrific. But mild fears show up in an actor's daydreams, and once in awhile a nightmare expresses worries about what can and does go wrong on stage. I know because I have worked in the theater for more than thirty-five years and was more recently involved in various stage productions in Maui as an actor, director, and performer of one-man productions. My usual nightmares feature minor mishaps like dropped lines, costume surprises, and worst of all memory lapses. Perhaps the events of the last few days made my dream so dark and dreadful.

As I lay in bed, recovering from the nightmare, I thought about real stage mishaps I was involved in. They were trivial compared to my dream, often humorous in retrospect, but not always. I remembered when I played Chief Sitting Bull in *Annie Get Your Gun*. I was to remove a large ceremonial necklace from my neck and place it on Annie Oakley's neck to symbolize her honorary membership in the tribe of which I was chief. I did this night after night, performance after performance without a hint of a problem. One night, however, when I put the necklace on her head and tugged it to get it in place, the string broke, and all the beads, bear claws, and bear teeth went clattering to the stage all around us. The audience began to titter, giggle, and then burst into laughter.

If one doesn't panic, I've found on stage and in life, it's possible to work through a tough situation. Actors learn how to cover up mistakes by being bold and inventive. In this case, I fell to my knees and began gathering the beads rolling around the stage, picking up bear teeth and claws, and proclaimed in an exaggerated dialect, "Ah, necklace broke. Must pick up beads. Give to Annie Oakley for present." The audience clapped in appreciation for the recovery.

It was comforting to think of this incident. It reminded me of who I was, and kept my mind off my situation in the hospital and the pain I was in. Other stage fiascoes came to mind. I recalled an incident that occurred before I even got on stage. I was performing one of my one-man shows playing the character of Mark Twain. It was one of several shows in my repertory that include *The Old Man and the Sea, A Child's Christmas in Wales,* an Einstein play, and C. S. Lewis.

This one particular performance was at an inn on Maui's west side with a spacious courtyard with flowering bushes, exotic trees, and tables and chairs. I was in costume, and putting on the last touches of makeup. The last thing to go on was the best part, an expensive, handmade, human-hair mustache. Because of Maui's humidity, the glue I used was the strongest available which I acquired after having embarrassing difficulties with a mustache coming partially unglued and flapping in the air while I tried to hold it in place with a handkerchief. I got the mustache on and patted down with a square of damp paper towel just as the stage manager told me to be ready for "places" in five minutes. Checking makeup in the mirror one last time, I realized that something was wrong. The mustache was inside out and upside down. I didn't know what to do. I slowly peeled it away careful not to tear it. I used solvent to get the glue off the mustache and my upper lip. Then I combed it, trimmed stray hairs, and reattached it. I was a wreck but eventually got it fixed, put on the white linen Twain coat, and walked over to the stage. Afterward, this awful event made me smile, although it didn't feel the least bit funny at the time.

While theater work and music gigs were my principal focus on Maui, it's not what brought me there in the first place. My wife and I had to move out of the carriage house we rented in Denver when the owner sold the property, and that got us thinking about where we wanted to go and what we wanted to do. We were looking for change and adventure. We decided to go to Maui because my daughter (by a previous marriage), and her family lived there. It felt like it was a good change for us, however we were only there a few months when another change came along.

A former university colleague and good friend contacted me and offered me a job teaching at a bilingual school in Colombia, where he had become an administrator. Off we went to Colombia. The first months in Santa Marta were an adventure trying to learn "survival" Spanish, fitting into a different culture, and teaching English in a K-12 Colombian school. My only teaching experience was at university. The elementary school children were quite a challenge, but somehow I persisted. After our commitment, we moved back to Maui. We had no other strong desires, and there were possibilities on the island, and sometimes Hawaii felt magical in contrast to years in Colorado.

My first job on Maui was playing music at restaurants, bars, and hotels. In time, I developed relationships with people in the theater community, and that led to acting and directing opportunities, as well as venues to perform the one-man shows that I had developed in Denver.

Theater work is full of challenges and risks and that's something that deeply appeals to me. I engage in several pursuits that can be challenging and sometimes frightening. It's not that I'm a daredevil or take what seems like unnecessary risks. But I like pushing myself and testing my endurance and have weathered numerous injuries. The worst was in the last high school football game of my senior year. I injured my spine and was in a body cast for four months.

I've been involved in various sports in my life including track, football, swimming, crossfit, distance running, skiing, and sailing. Never great at any of them, but they gave me confidence, meaning, joy, and many memorable experiences. Climbing mountains became a passion in my twenties. I've done technical climbing and guiding, but as the birthdays have accumulated, enjoyment now is a challenging hike to a mountain top requiring no equipment but plenty of endurance. Growing up in Colorado, I was fortunate to have a variety of opportunities to enjoy the wonders and the challenges of the high mountains. Hiking up mountains is part of my life, something that I try to do as often as I can when conditions and opportunities allow. On Maui, my theater work and music left me time to pursue other interests including hiking Haleakala's crater trails. It was, of course, on just such a hike that landed me in the predicament I was in, lying in a hospital bed, consumed by pain all over my body, and having come so perilously close to death. Lying there, I went over in my mind all the events that led me to where I was.

CHAPTER 3

BEGINNING

I carry a waist pack to the car. It has a zippered top compartment with nylon loops on either side for the two water bottles. My light-weight boots are tied loosely on my feet. I wear a favorite baseball cap, yellow with a buckle in the back to adjust the size, no advertising anywhere on it. I throw the pack into the back seat and drive through the parking lot of the three-story Hale Ono Loa buildings. My wife and I rent a studio apartment here. The air smells sweet with the fresh blossoms of plumeria trees. Our apartment fronts the ocean, and as I drive toward the driveway, I turn and look between the buildings where the light sparkles on a breaking wave. It occurs to me that my drive up to Haleakala begins at a sea-level parking lot, and will end at the Halemau'u trailhead parking lot at eight thousand feet.

It's a two-and-a-half-hour drive from our place in Honokawai, through Lahaina, and then east on the single-lane highway to the "other side" where the adjacent towns of Kahului, the commercial center of Maui, and Wailuku where the county and state government offices are found. Usually, I leave earlier, 6:30 or so, for Haleakala. This morning, I take my time leaving at 10:00. In the early morning, the highway has heavy traffic leading into Lahaina, mostly workers who service resorts and high-end homes on the west side of the island. The other lane leading to Kahului has little traffic.

At this later hour, both directions of the highway are busy. I tell myself to resist the temptation to get angry at people who drive slowly and take in the view along the coast that sometimes includes humpback whales. I should be patient. They're visitors, and when they see the deep blue of the ocean before a wave breaks, becoming whiter than white, it is spell-binding and doesn't diminish with multiple views. When I visit other places and take in the sights, I hear the horns of impatient locals. Even here there are times when I slow down my old car to gaze out of the passenger side window toward the Big Island of Hawaii. On a rare day, I can make out the upper slopes of its Mauna Loa and Mauna Kea volcanoes. I see them shimmering, but a honking horn shakes me from gazing too long

On the outskirts of Kahului, I make a right turn, then a quick left onto a shortcut road that takes me to the highway that climbs up along Haleakala's massive flank. Right after the turn, a pungent odor seeps through the open window. Many people are annoyed by the smell, but I welcome it as a reminder of the only remaining sugar factory on Maui. The shortcut ends with a right turn onto a four-lane highway that grows steeper past the towns of Pukalani on the right, and Makawao on the left. Another turn puts me on the Haleakala Highway that gives magical views of the pastures where today horses range and cattle find shade, water, and grass. I smell the sweet grasses and marvel at the Jacaranda trees that are now in purple bloom.

Along the highway at an altitude of about three thousand feet, is the Kula Inn Lodge and Restaurant. A steep driveway leads to the Kula Marketplace, the last outpost for food and drinks. Kula is a town of sorts spread over a large area without many services. I always stop at the Kula Marketplace to buy food for the hike. Each time I get out of the car there, I'm dazzled at the grandeur of the West Maui Mountains across the valley, and the Pacific glimmering on both sides of the Island. The glory of it is always a surprise.

My lunch purchases at the store are the same each time I'm here: turkey and cheese and peanut butter and jelly sandwiches, chips, an apple, and a couple of energy bars. It would be cheaper to buy lunch fixings at a grocery store in Lahaina near home, but I prefer to stop up here for the view. I grab a coffee for the drive to the top and ruin it with vanilla cream, a treat. Stepping outside, I sit on the steps of the store looking at the heavy clouds that hang low at timberline as usual in the rising elevation. Rain is predicted for this evening. That's not unusual either. I'm not worried about the weather. I know it's a late start and not the wisest time to head off, but I've hiked several trails in the crater. I can move quickly if the need presents itself. I've done it many times. When a thunderstorm grows over a mountain peak, I hustle down into the trees for safety. Though I am in my mid-sixties, my health is excellent, and I have much experience.

I'm feeling stiff, so it's time to get going. I eat one sandwich in the car on the way up because I haven't had breakfast and save the other for lunch on the trail. Driving along I turn the radio on and hear Israel Kamakawiwoʻole, called "Iz," an icon of Hawaiian music, performing his landmark rendition of "Over the Rainbow." As many times as I've listened to the song, and as many times as I've performed it myself, it still touches me. I added it to my repertoire years ago. While Maui is my home, and I have some music gigs here, when I return to Colorado I play several days a week at Creekside Cellars. Creekside is a winery/restaurant in Evergreen a foothills town near Denver. I sing a variety of songs: pop, urban folk, songs from musical theater, jazz standards, and some original music. I accompany myself on guitar, and play jazz flute to background rhythm tracks. It is a home away from home with dear people I love to see.

Iz's song brought back a poignant memory of an afternoon when a woman stumbled awkwardly through the door of the restaurant, a caregiver holding her tightly around the waist, and an older man following closely behind. It was clear that the woman was suffering from a serious health condition. As I performed, a strong impulse drew me to their table to sing to her, but I wondered if it would be proper. Would it offend her or her husband? And what should I sing? As I was finishing my set, it occurred to me to sing "Over the Rainbow" to her. I walked over to the table, sat down, and began singing. As soon as I started, I feared it was a terrible choice, but I continued, and they seemed engaged in it. Some weeks later her husband returned to the restaurant and told me that his wife had died, and he wanted me to know how much it meant to her that I had sung that song. He continued to say that he bought an album of mine with "Over the Rainbow" on it, and his wife listened to it often during the last few days of her life.

The song on the radio had ended, and I turned off the radio because I was caught up in another memory of performing at the restaurant. Two couples, one older and one younger sat down at a table near me. Between songs, the young man, wearing a suit and tie and sporting a boutonniere came over to me and requested a particular John Denver song, which I didn't know. I suggested another song that I thought might be similar, and he was delighted. I asked him what the occasion was, and he replied that he and the young lady had just gotten married. I asked when and he said, "About ten minutes ago at my parent's home," nodding towards the older couple at the table. Shy as I can sometimes be, it occurred to me that it might be a nice gesture to go and sit at their table, and sing the song just to them. As I sang, I saw tears flowing down the cheeks of the young man and his wife. I was stirred at being allowed to provide such a simple but meaningful gift for them.

I might have gone on with more memories of this kind, but I was nearing my destination. Two trails lead into the crater from this side of Haleakala. The Sliding Sands Trail begins just below the summit at a parking lot on the northwest corner of the crater and descends into the crater's west side. Once at the bottom, the trail is mostly flat and leads to a guest cabin and beyond. The other trailhead, the Halemau'u, begins at the parking lot six miles before the summit. Instead of going down into the crater and then back up the same way, hikers can make a loop inside the crater either by going down the Sliding Sands Trail, around the crater, and then up and out on the Halemau'u trail, or the reverse. Either way, unless a group has two cars, they have to hitchhike at the beginning of the hike or at the end. I decide to park at the lower Halemau'u lot and hitch a ride up to the parking lot near the Sliding Sands trailhead. There's a hitch-hiker's lane across from the parking lot on the highway to the top. Hopefully, I'll get a ride. I always have, but sometimes it takes a while. Many visitors look the other way as they go by.

I drive into the Halemau'u lot and park, the only car. That's odd. It's the first time I've seen it empty. I pause a moment. I notice the clouds hanging low and a breezy chill when I get out of the decrepit '97 Corolla. Such a vehicle is called a "Maui Cruiser" on the Island. I open the back door to sit and put on two pairs of socks and then tug on my shoes. The cell phone reads, 1:45. I decide to leave the phone in the car. I figure it might fall out of my pocket, especially if I have to jog at some point.

No room in the waist pack even for a cell phone. I put on the waist pack, buckle it, and cinch it tight. The water bottles are snug in their nylon straps. I wrestle the pack around to the front of me so I can stuff in the food. I go light because I like to move quickly. I carry all I need and no more. I crinkle up the plastic sandwich box as small as possible and stuff it in the pack. It's the turkey and cheese, though it may not look like that when I pull it out to eat. On top of the sandwich, I shove in the apple, two energy bars, and then snack on small bag of chips.

It takes some doing, but I manage to cram in my ancient yellow windbreaker. Zipping it tight is a challenge. Then I tie an old rag-ged sweatshirt around my waist beneath the pack, and I'm set.

I wear heavy white cotton painter's pants with loops on either side. I found them at a Goodwill store a few days earlier. They're cool looking and comfortable if a little heavy. Usually, I wear khaki shorts, but I thought the painter's pants would be good for today if the temperature dropped because the forecasted rain comes later this afternoon. I suppose they are odd for hiking, but I like them. They're sturdy. I wear another Goodwill treasure, a T-shirt without advertising. I loathe wearing a signboard showing I ran some race twenty-five years ago or advertising products.

There is one exception to the advertising ban, and that's the sweatshirt with a monogram on the front that reads *Eaglebrook*. It's an old friend of mine that I've worn playing touch football, climbing, and doing chores. *Eaglebrook* is an eastern prep school, and the sweatshirt was a gift from a teacher there. He and I were instructors at Outward Bound some forty years before, which explains its vintage look and tattered condition. I'll never get rid of it.

I have a penchant for wearing gloves on a hike, partly because of an unsubstantiated belief that they keep my hands from swelling, but they do protect my hands if I need to pull myself up some boulders or walk through prickly bushes. For years, my gloves of choice have been cowhide work gloves. This morning I couldn't find them, so I grabbed a pair of denim gardening gloves. I figured they'd do.

I put on my yellow baseball cap, sunglasses, and gloves. The wind's up with a chill, but I keep the windbreaker in the pack and the sweatshirt around my waist. The T-shirt will be enough once I get moving. Walking across the highway to the hitchhiker's pullover lane, two Nene waddle right for me. They are a species of goose endemic to Hawaii, and like all geese, they are beggars. They honk loudly at me and increase their pace. They want a snack. I stare down at them, shaking my head, unwilling to dig through my crammed pack for a morsel. I feel no guilt. I need all I'm carrying. They keep up the racket, but I'm unmoved. I sidle around them and hustle toward the lane, hopeful for a short wait for a ride.

Smiling with gratitude, I hold my thumb out for twenty minutes and watch thirteen cars slow and then accelerate past me. I begin to wonder if any helpful driver will pull over. Another ten minutes pass. I'm walking in little circles putting out my thumb when I hear a car laboring around the curve. This one stops, backs up, and the couple inside gives me a warm smile. I take off the waist pack and get into the back seat thanking them profusely for stopping, and we introduce ourselves to each other. They hail from New Zealand and have never been to Maui. An affable conversation begins, full of touristy questions and my long-winded answers. I guess my gratitude for the ride expresses itself in far more verbiage than they ask for or want. After handshakes at the Visitor Center parking lot, they head for the nearby stone shelter crammed with tourists. I head for a path where a worn wooden sign indicates the beginning of the Sliding Sands Trail.

The sand doesn't slide, although I suppose that with a fast start, there may be a place or two where a running leap might make for a slide. The trail is well marked and tamped down by years of hikers. I like the variety of taking different trails in the crater and have never had a problem.

The view into the crater from the start of the Sliding Sands is spectacular. A wide-open vista appears Mars-like. Otherworldly. Ancient. Whatever the comparison, everyone agrees that it is breathtaking. Each time I stand here, I am in awe of a multitude of cinder cones colored red, black, ochre, gray, and white. The surface is a desert, and the rugged rim has points that look like they belong in the Rocky Mountains. This part of the crater is barren. Further on, toward the other end, the crater grows lush with vegetation. The wind is picking up, so with a shiver, I start down, glancing at the sky for potential trouble. Clouds lightly stir above. I pull my cap tightly on my head, slip on the gloves, and begin the more than two thousand-foot descent to the crater floor. I'll be sweating as soon as the crater walls block the wind, and the pace warms me.

A small group of crestfallen hikers struggles uphill toward me. Going down the trail is easy with much to look at and talk about; going back up is a shock and a struggle. Further on, a young couple wearing sandals walks a few steps. He stops to shake out the sand.

He looks at me with a broad smile and calls out a pleasant, "Hi." Behind him, his companion struggles up, blindly staring at her bruised toes in silence. A few minutes later, I swing around a switchback nearly colliding with two older women who pay me no mind, chattering loudly as they make their way up with the aid of trekking poles. At the bottom, the path levels, and I pick up the pace under the west wall of the rim toward the Kapalaoa cabin. This is one of three cabins that nestle in the crater for those who want to spend a night or longer. No camping is allowed anywhere in the crater except in these well-outfitted cabins. Reservations must be made for a stay--usually three months in advance.

CHAPTER 4

MOVE

AS the Kapalaoa cabin comes into view, I notice two couples sitting on either side of the trail. I pull my cap down so that all I can see are my boots and pick up the pace. Stopping to chat while moving quickly on a trail is a rarity for me. I might nod, even smile, as I quickly plow ahead into the sought-after quiet.

"Aren't you cold?" one of the girls pipes up. They're all bundled in parkas.

Without slowing, I look over my shoulder as I pass them and quip, "No, I'm hot. Got a long way to go."

I don't often stop and talk with people I meet on the trail, although I'd certainly stop if someone was in trouble and needed help. I usually greet fellow hikers with a "Hi," or "Steep hill," but rarely stop. If someone stops to talk, I'll chat briefly but move as soon as I can. I'm shy, and I also want to keep moving. I feel a little guilty about it and know it's a bit selfish, but my mind is on my goal. For whatever reason, I'm driven.

As I go past the couples, I turn and look over my shoulder lifting my gloved hands and shout, "See, I've got my work gloves on. I've got to work in my garden down here." I feel guilty about how really weird this must sound. I should go back and talk with them to erase any bad impressions I may have made. They seemed like nice young people. I look skyward at abundant clouds hanging lower than a half-hour ago. The breeze is freshening. Not a good idea to tarry, and I move on. I drove a long way to come here, and I'm determined to complete the hike I planned. I'll just have to hustle and not waste any time if I don't want to get drenched.

I reach the Kapalaoa Cabin quickly. I don't know the time because I left my phone in the car and don't have a watch. I feel some concern. The trail I'm on continues on ahead for three miles to the Piluku cabin. But here, where I am, three trails cut across to the other side of the crater to pick up the Halemau'u trail without having to go to the Paliku cabin. I don't want to get caught down here under these growing clouds.

I need to eat and drink before I cross over to the Halemau'u trail that will take me to the Holua cabin and then out of the crater. I don't sit to eat because rest wastes time. I must keep moving. I wrestle to get the food out of my stuffed waist pack. I unzip and forage for one of the protein bars and pull out one of the water bottles from a loop, but drink sparingly. Keeping my head down, I don't look at the sky. I don't want to know what I know without looking. The sky closes in with mist I can feel. Time to move and quickly. The bar's gone in a few bites, and then I take another sip while starting across the crater floor. My heart pounds with fear because I know the trails that cross here get sketchy. The air smells heavier. There will be rain. I hope later rather than sooner.

I choose the trail that passes between the two cinder cones, Pu'u Nole and Pu'u Naue. I've taken this path several times on previous hikes. It's the shortest, but I have also lost this trail in the sand and small gullies only to find it after ten or fifteen minutes. The other trails remain obvious. Still, it will cost precious time if I take one of them. This one is the quickest way, and if I can keep from losing it, it will save time and allow me to walk quickly instead of having to run. My breath comes deep and fast, drying my throat. Water would taste so good, but I can't drink it now because I might need the water later.

Soon I wonder if this is the best way. Did I make the wrong choice? I shake my head and talk out loud, "Pay attention! Don't lose the trail!" Sweat stains my T-shirt front and back. I look up. I can't help it. The clouds have darkened, and the wind picks up. Not good. Run!

I run. Weariness overcomes me quickly. I know I can't run all the way to the Holua cabin. So, I stop for a moment's breath and then start again alternating between a jog and a fast walk. My voice is hoarse but loud, "Don't stop!" Suddenly, the trail disappears. I stop and anxiously search for it. I remember there's a short descent here and the trail should be visible rising ahead. I find it, and with palpable relief, stumble onto the Halemau'u trail, turn, and head toward Holua cabin which is tucked beneath a portion of the crater's rim. The light behind the clouds begins to dim. It would feel good to make it to the cabin before dark; because from there it's only a half-an-hour to the where trail goes up and outside the rim on a series of switchbacks. It's very steep, but once I get there, I'm only a mile from the car on a less steep route. It's an arduous climb but worth it for the rest at the end.

Halfway to the cabin, I can't run anymore. There's a small sign ahead on the side of the trail. I recognize the place from many passes by here. "Silversword Loop," it announces, pointing toward a path that begins to circle, rejoining the main trail of the Halemau'u a quarter mile beyond where I am. I've swept past this sign many times at a steady pace. At other times, I stopped and spent time looking at the Silversword plants a few steps behind the sign. The plants are in different stages of development and are as mysterious as they are beautiful. They only bloom once and then die soon after. Long life and then a rapid end.

The wind picks up, and my back dries with a shiver. I must move, though I'd like to sit down and chew an apple and take a drink. I can't. I have to carry on quickly. I walk faster and then break into an unsteady jog.

I reach Holua cabin and bend over a few moments, gasping for air. After I catch my breath, I begin a slow jog toward the wall where the trail will rise. Halfway there is not much light left, but I'm close to the switchbacks that go up and will lead me out of the crater. I can feel the tall grass in my hands as I spread them from my sides to keep track of the trail. The familiar smell of green grass is comforting. My anxiety lessens with the closeness of getting up and out of here. I'm not worried now, as I start up the narrow pathway of switchbacks against the rock wall. I've been here before. I know I'll be protected from the strong wind and the rain sure to follow. I see the cliff and begin stepping up the rock-cobbled path that is just one person wide. A fall from here could be a sudden death, or at least broken bones far off the trail.

I'm confident even though darkness falls like a curtain. I can't see the tops of my boots—only my gloved hands are visible. I feel the wind and rain intensify, but the rock wall protects me. Feeling my way along the wall, my ascent slows. The discomfort doesn't hold fear. I step slowly, sure that I will be okay. At last, I know I'm nearing the top of the crater because I feel the path turning the broad corner and the safety of a gradual slope toward the parking lot. It will be safe even if it's a mud-sloppy walk. I know exactly where I am, and all is well.

CHAPTER 5

CHAOS

AS I edge around this final corner, suddenly a head-on blast of torrential rain hits me. The gale drives me back a couple of steps and then to my knees. I bury my head between my legs. In a matter of moments, I'm soaked to the skin. I murmur for help. I untie the sweatshirt around my waist and tug it on over my sopping T-shirt. The trail is no more visible here than against the black wall. It's a sheet of rain. Reaching out to each side of the trail, I feel the large stones that line it. When I stand, I can't see anything of the trail. I need a flashlight to show the stone borders of the trail, but I don't have one. I'm disoriented, and my eyes are nearly closed against this violence. Why didn't I bring a flashlight? I don't even have one in the car.

"I'm okay," I tell myself. "Just bend over and walk" I kick against the stones on either side of the trail to stay in the middle of it. I can make it this way. I'm in control. I can stumble up this trail. I know this place. Only a mile. Even if it takes an hour, I know I'll soon be in the old Toyota heading down the Haleakala highway, heater blasting, and leaning toward coffee and a sweet roll at the Kula Marketplace.

My progress slows to only a few steps at a time. I fall headfirst into prickly bushes off to the side of the path, and my hands sting with tiny punctures. I stand quickly and take a few steps then slip on pebbles and fall back on my butt with such a jolt that tears come to my eyes. I lean over on my side and rub the pain. The thought that I am very close to the parking lot tempers my pain. After a long day's hike, it is always a weary walk back to the car. It's easy to underestimate the distance back to the starting place.

I remember that this stretch of trail has three or four steep hairpin turns going up that swing perilously close to the edge of the crater walls where hikers pause to take photos across the vista to other parts of the rim and cinder cones below. I know that in this storm, I could come to one of those lookouts and step right over the edge, a thousand-foot chasm. As I stumble, again and again, I'm obsessed with the certainty that I will fall to my death if I don't abandon this trail. I get a flash of insight. There's a fence to the right of the trail along here. It must be close, very close. The fence stands four to five feet tall with steel strands weaving vertically and horizontally attaching to metal posts dug deep into the volcanic soil. Of course, the fence isn't visible, but I know I can run into it if I turn off the trail now, and I turn. I shiver violently. The temperature has dropped without my noticing. Now I notice.

Without warning, I bump into the fence. Though my hands are soaked and numb inside the soggy denim gloves, I grab hold of the top wire. I begin to shuffle along the fence line in the same direction I was trying to walk up, but I know that soon the fence makes a sharp turn into one of the deep valleys of a rainforest. I can only follow the fence for a short time. I'll have to leave the fence there and climb back up to the trail. I'm sure I'll be past the danger of the trail I was on that comes close the edge of the crater wall. Within a short time, the fence does turn sharply, and I leave it walking some, but mostly crawling until I am stopped by a thicket of bushes. I sit down, struggling to pull off the treasured but sopping wet sweatshirt. When it slops off, I angrily throw it as far away as I can. I don't know why I do that. Frustration. My T-shirt is soaked, but for some reason I think it will be okay to leave it on because it's lightweight. I zip open the pack and dig out the thin orange windbreaker that I have forgotten has no water repellent quality whatsoever. The protein bar, apple, and peanut butter and jelly sandwich fall to the rain soaked ground when I tug on the windbreaker. The plastic sandwich box must have broken earlier because the sandwich lies in the water soggy, uneatable. The waist pack is now empty. I fling off a glove and grope on the ground to find the food. When I do, I stuff what's left back into the pack. The water bottles hang in their loops, one full, the other half empty because I took a drink when I paused at the first cabin. It seems I drank more than I thought before crossing the crater.

The pack contains no knife, compass, map, matches, extra clothing, waterproof jacket, or food besides the apple and the remaining protein bar. The small pack, snug around my waist, can't hold much. As I said, I like to travel light. Though drenched, I crave water, so I take two sips and then two more. I'm sure I'll be at the car soon and be able to get food and water, but I decide to keep the other bottle full just in case.

Sitting there, I yell out at the top of my lungs, "I'm freezing." The ancient windbreaker is like a sieve. I miss the sweatshirt. It seems to me now that it would have been good to have its soggy bulk. Even wet it gave me warmth. My mind races. My voice rises again. "Why did I throw it away?" I must get out of here. I stand up and start again even though the torrent pounds against me. I need to turn my back to it now and then.

I struggle to walk upward to find the trail. Time and again, my toes slam against large rocks I can't see. Bushes trip me, and I fall forward into them. I convince myself with the thought that the parking lot must be below me. I'm sure of it. I've been going up and up for a long time up. I missed the parking lot! It's got to be below me now. Below me and to the right. I convince myself that I have gone way too high and too far to the left which means that I'm again back up near the rim. Looking back now, these were the first of many delusions I would have in the hours to come.

Firmly convinced that the way to safety is down and to the right, I stumble along trying to keep as level as I can before I decide to start down. Panic guides me. The tangled brush thins, the rain has slowed, and I can see ahead for the first time since I hiked up the switchbacks into the gale. I see a few trees in the distance and boulders. The rain plays games with me, gaining speed. I duck my head in the blasts. When it slows, I look up and see in the distance something large. It must be a huge boulder, and I think maybe there's a cave. Once again, the wind picks up, and I push against it toward the boulder, toward the safety and the warmth that is inside its cave.

It is not a boulder with a cave. It's a tree. No matter, I crumple against the trunk under a canopy of skimpy limbs. Grateful for any protection, a feeling of friendship for the tree comes over me. I'm safe here. I calm down, calm my shaking body and tangle of thoughts. I dig out a protein bar and the nearly empty water bottle. I drain it and then bite off a chunk of the bar. I lean my head against the tree trunk gazing through the limbs.

The rain slows. Through the branches a small window opens in the clouds where the moon shines through. I wrap my arms around myself to try for warmth. I'm encouraged, and so my mind wanders off to another time and place. In my mind, I see a sailboat pushing through the ocean. I am several miles out in a rented thirty-two-foot sailboat with two paying guests. Anchoring off of a tiny islet, I turn off the engine and jump into the dark blue sea. The sun begins to descend, and it's time to head back. After I dry off, I start the engine. That is, I try to start it, but it doesn't even turn over after countless tries.

There's nothing to be done about it except to set sail. We need to get back to San Diego before dark. About halfway back, a sudden realization hits me. How can I get into the designated slip without an engine? I have to fire up the engine and take down the sails, but, of course, the engine won't fire up. Both batteries are dead. The obvious solution is to call the harbor patrol on the radio. They'll arrange for a commercial towboat to fetch us.

But when I get to the San Diego harbor, I don't call for a tow. I'm embarrassed about doing so. I don't want to look incompetent in front of the experts—an idiot who shouldn't be out on the ocean at all. So, I make a plan. In the coming dusk, I know that the wind will slow and come in from the west. My slip is a boat-wide parking place on the water, along with hundreds of other boats. Mine faces west. Sailing east with the wind behind me from the west, I can turn a hundred and eighty degrees into the light breeze, and the boat might slow just enough not to do much damage, and that's what I do.

When I got close to the dock, I take off my shirt and pants and wearing only my swim trunks, and I run up to the bow and grab the line tied there. Taking the free end, I wrap a couple of turns around my wrist. I figure that if I don't make it all the way in, or if the boat is moving too quickly, I can jump into the water and tie the bow to one of the large posts anchored at the end of each slip. Back at the wheel, I make a turn down the lane with only a boat's width on either side. Then, with another quick turn, I steer directly into the slip. I ready myself to jump into the water. The sailboat creeps in, slowed by the facing breeze, and stops a foot from the dock. I step off the boat onto the dock and am greeted by the clapping of several sailors standing nearby.

I realize that I'm thinking of this story because I'm hoping for a similar outcome. Now, as then, my predicament is due partly to pride, stubbornness, and dread of being viewed as less than competent. I feel okay. I can get out of this mess.

CHAPTER 6

HOPE

I look down the slope below me. Lights are glowing. I know those lights. They're streetlights, a shopping center, baseball fields, and dim car headlights. It's Kahului, and next to it is Wailuku Town. Nearer, I can see the Haleakala highway winding down in front of the other, lower Visitor's Center close to the Park entrance. Next to it the ranger station glows under a light hung on its outside wall. I am certain my car is just below me, hidden below a bulge in the slope. It can't be more than a mile. I'm safe now.

I stand up painfully and stiffly. Relief quenches my needs. I begin searching down the slope for the parking lot. I can't see it yet, but I'm positive it's there. All I need to do is go straight down this slope, and I'll run right into it. Then there will be the warmth of the car and a phone call to assure Kimberly that I'm fine. I'll just be getting home a little later. What could be better than just heading for those lights? With the light of the moon, all I have to do is hike straight down. I'll come to the road and then I can walk comfortably on the asphalt to the ranger station---no thought of the parking lot.

The rain has stopped, and the clouds are lined in the moon's light. I can't believe how bad it was, and how good it is now. I start down but find the mountainside steeper than I thought. Ruts in the lava again cause me to stumble, and several times I fall face down, catching myself on my elbows or rolling on my side. Ahead,

29

I can see something deeper than a rut and the moonlight doesn't show the bottom of it. I realize that this may not be as easy as I thought. I must be careful. There are ravines and sinkholes. I try to be careful, but I step into one and it's a shock even if it's only a foot deep. There's no warning. When they're deeper, I bang against the side and crumple at the bottom. I climb out in disbelief that I'm still conscious.

The shivering returns not from the cold, but from a new fear, a fear that I could be badly hurt falling like this. My cranky legs move like the Tin Man. Fear pumps me with energy, and I move as quickly as I can. Still, I fall into ravines that are over my head. My confidence about getting to the town lights falters. Could I even get to the ranger station only a couple of miles away? Sometimes, when I can make out an opening in the ground, I climb down inside it and then climb up out the other side. The idea of the parking lot comes to me again. I had forgotten, but I know it's nearby. The town lights wait for me. The ranger station light waits for me. The car waits.

The faraway lights dim. A misty gauze creeps over the moon. The moonlight fades and then disappears behind the now heavy clouds. Everything disappears. The towns are gone, the valley, and the ranger station. When I look all around me, a dark, thick mist blocks everything, including my hope.

And then the rain returns rushing as if from an open faucet. Once more, I can't even see the tops of my boots. I shake with the cold. I know I must keep moving down, but I also know I must be very careful. Falls into unseen holes await me. Carefully, I walk down and then, without warning, step into the air of a dark hole. In an instant, there's the scraping sound of soles on the black wall. My head bangs against it. For a moment I'm senseless, and then throw up on the unseen lava floor. I turn around, lie down, and fall asleep.

When I wake, I know I must climb out and keep going, but first I need water, only a sip from the almost empty bottle. When I reach for it, the belt loop is empty. I kneel and search for it with my hand, dragging my palm back and forth along the bottom. I check the loops. One loop holds the full bottle, but the other loop is empty. I crawl around again, scraping my hands against the lava. I need my gloves. I put them in my back pocket at the tree to unwrap the energy bar. When I reach around to my back pockets, there are no gloves. One more time, with a pounding heart, I sweep with both hands. I can't believe it. Where are they? The water bottle's gone; the gloves are gone. With a pang of fear, I reach across the belt pack for the loop and touch the full bottle. I sit with my back to the wall and console myself that I have this one full bottle of water and the road is close-by. I'm okay without the gloves. The road is just below. The moon may come out again, and the valley lights will shine. I know I can't keep falling like this, banging my head. No one will find me in here. I stand up and struggle out of the hole.

It's much colder now. The rain continues heavy. It would feel so good to go back down into the ravine. Warmer in there, and I could sleep. I want to lie down because I feel sick and weary. Violent shivering shakes me out of this brief fantasy. I know that I must keep moving to keep warm, to find safety. I tell myself to take slow, careful steps, and suddenly I crash down into a sinkhole and hit my knee hard. I can't do this anymore.

An idea comes to me that if I turn to the right here, and walk as level as I can across the slope, I'll come to another part of the boundary fence sooner than I would trying to get to the ranger station, and maybe safer. It's part of the fence that surrounds the entire Park, and this part runs down to the Hosmer Grove Campground. If I can get to that fence, I can hold on to it and shuffle down to the campground. It will be safe holding on to the fence. I'll get out of here. Again, a trickle of hope seeps inside me, even though I shiver and stumble.

While moving across the hillside, I find there are fewer ravines and sinkholes. Prickly bushes scratch me at times, and small hills make it difficult to keep a level contour, but none of these things frighten me. It's so much better than all that has gone before. My mind is sharper than it's been. Even though I still cannot see more than a few feet in front of me, my hope for the fence keeps me moving. I waver. I should be at the fence by now. It's worrisome, but there is nothing I can do except move toward where I guess it stands.

I see the wire strands before my chest hits the fence. My bare hands grasp the wire with elation. Here it is. I reach over to a post and try to wiggle it to see if it's strong. It is. I can only see the fence a foot or two in each direction. Everywhere else it is hidden. No matter. I'm sure that this great fence will lead me down this slope right into Hosmer Grove. Campers will be there with warm blankets, food, cell phones, and most important of all, water. All I have to do is face the fence and walk sideways with my hands on the top strand of wire to guide me and protect me from stumbling. I take a few sideways steps. What a relief!

In an instant, my feet fly off the ground. I'm hanging mid-air with bare hands gripping the thin steel wire. I look down between my boots and there is only impenetrable darkness. I have no idea of what's beneath me or how deep it is. Whatever adrenaline remains floods my body. I stretch my toes to try to touch something below, but there is nothing. I can't hold myself any longer. I must get back to the ground, where I stood only a step or two away. I swing my body back in that direction. Ever so slightly, the tips of my boots touch the ground, but I can't stand up because my body leans to where the ground falls away. I try again, knowing this may be my last swing. Gratefully, I stand on firm ground, exhausted. The strain on my hands grows into a cramp. My shoulders ache from the weight of soaked-through clothing. I know I can't go hand-over-hand down the wire. I can't go up either. It's too steep. I'm too weary. I bend over to catch my breath and decide to hold on to the wire and step to where I hung a moment ago and let go. I have a vague idea that it can't be too much of a drop because it's along the fence. I massage my protesting hands and then grip the top wire, taking the two side steps to where I hang. I climb down each strand of wire until I hold the last wire in both hands. I let go.

CHAPTER 7

Despair and Dream

WHEN I come to, I'm lying on my back in the mud. Rain splatters my face and body. The worthless windbreaker, T-shirt, cotton pants, and socks stick to me coated with drizzling mud on my backside. I reach up to pull my baseball cap over my eyes. It's gone. A dank smell nauseates me. My head throbs. I lean on an elbow, tilt my mouth into the rain, and try to drink. Without success. When I stand, darkness invades everywhere. I take feeble steps. The tall grass is drenched and slick. Inching down sideways, I hold the grass with both hands, often to no avail. Falling is a habit. I feel the clumps of bushes among the grass that prickle against my legs. Once again, I'm on my backside sliding down the slope. I stop, dazed, and hear the sound of water nearby. When I get up, I hear the water from one direction, and silence from the other. Perhaps a brook fills a pool, and that is where the sound stops.

A new thought comes to me. Creeks always go downhill. In Colorado, if a hiker gets turned around and can't find a way out, the best course of action is to follow a stream downhill. They flow and eventually come to a valley and a road. The danger is that cliffs often line the sides of flowing water, and danger lurks there. I don't think of that. I only think that if this brook flows out of the pond, then I can follow it to the highway where there are people. I can get a ride into Kahului. I turn toward the vague outline of the pond and hear the trickling sound of water. It's overgrown here, and I fall to my knees. Reaching a hand into the water, I touch the shallow bottom of a brook that must come out of the pool. I can walk on the pebbles of the brook. I think of nothing, not even bending down for a drink of water. I simply follow this shallow brook that will lead me to the highway and home.

I don't remember the fall under the fence, nor the slip-sliding down through the foliage. I'm only aware of walking on the stones at the bottom of the brook, just a few inches deep. I haven't a clue where I am. My attention is focused on plodding down the brook to the safety of the highway. I don't think about how far it might be or what obstacles might stand in the way.

Later, I find out that I am no longer in Haleakala National Park. And I learn that this stream does not intersect the Hana Highway for at least ten miles, with a descent of five thousand feet through dense forest, waterfalls, deep gullies, and cliffs. I stumble now and then, but no matter, I'm moving somewhere. I could be sleepwalking.

I'm suddenly falling backward. My right shoulder hits a rock, then my head whips back and slams against a wall of rock. I hear my only water bottle bounce off a wall below me, then splash into the water. My left boot wedges in a crack and when I try to get up, I cannot stand. By moving my foot back and forth, the boot finally comes free, and I fall into a pool of freezing, chest-deep water. When I look around, all I can see is the dark outline of a wall in front of me. I wade through the water, pulling with my outstretched hands. My toes and hands hit the rock wall at the same time. There is a shelf there a foot or so above the water level at my chest. I'm trembling with cold and fear. I must get out.

I place my arms flat on top of the shelf and try to push myself up out of the water. I grope for a nub or crack under the water to wedge a boot into, but only reach up a few inches because my waterlogged clothes hold me down like an anchor. I try again and again, each time a frightful failure. I lift the other leg higher and probe, but the underwater wall is as vertical and smooth as the water itself. I try to jump several times and fling my arms on the flat rock to push up. It's futile. My boots don't even lift off the bottom now. I count four tries, then lay my head on the flat shelf in front of me. No one will ever find me here. I'm not getting out of this water. I don't know what to do.

I shake violently. "God help me." In a vague dullness my emotions vacillate between fear and hope, confusion and anxiety that repeat in a convoluted circle over and over again. My thoughts, when they clear, are consumed with survival. Survival would be a gift.

My boots scrape wildly on the straight wall. I dig my fingers into the grit on the shelf. In a moment, I am lying face down in mud and rocks. I'm out of the pool. Sobs shake my weary body. I roll over on my back. The rain has slowed. I fall asleep and into a deep dream of a mountain and a brook.

* * *

In the dream, I'm in Colorado. I kick my boots deep into the sand and rocks to keep from sliding backwards. Sometimes I slip a few feet and then start again, sweating profusely. I make it to the boulders where the sliding pebbles end. I can make my way more quickly now, though the altitude gain often has me stopping for a breath. It's been over two hours climbing above the timberline on this peak, and the reward of the top can't be far. With all the effort of going up, it's a comfort to know that going down will be easier. I will follow the sun as it descends in the west.

After some false summits, I climb up one more massive boulder to the top. There's a light, cool breeze and views that delight me, as they do each time I go up high. I walk around in a circle to take in the vista. There are several peaks over fourteen thousand feet in this range. I've climbed a few of them and hope for more. I slide the pack off of my shoulders, looking for a flat rock to sit on and another to lean against. Rarely am I that lucky, but I find a place that works. A perfect day surrounds me.

I like going solo. It gives me a chance to think about all sorts of things. Sometimes an inner dialogue takes place about which way to go, and when to rest and snack. Sometimes I hum a song to keep rhythm with the movement or think about what I'm going to tell friends about today's hike. I also welcome hiking with companions. Going it alone doesn't bring the gifts of the many conversations along the forest trails, making joint decisions about the way up, sharing the summit, complaining about the descent, and finally rehearsing the day's glory on the way home. I've shared these adventures with many companions over many years. Just out of high school I attended the Colorado Outward Bound School and learned much about mountaineering. Later I became an instructor there, and then a guide in Rocky Mountain National Park. It has been a gift for me to introduce young and old alike to adventuresome experiences.

It's time to go because I feel a growing stiffness in my legs. Stooping to retrieve the pack strains my back muscles, so I hold the pack against my chest and move back and forth and up and down a few times. I head down to the opposite side of the mountain. In a few minutes, I come to a narrow snow-filled gully that is soft on top and firm underneath. It's a great place to glissade down, skiing on my boots with an ice-ax in hand to steer or stop a fall. The gully makes an S-turn opening into a wide meadow. In the middle of it, glistens a brook weaving between tall green grasses.

I come to a place where the water crosses through the meadow. I take off my cap, lie down on my stomach over the water, and plunge my head deep into it. Without a pause, I drink until choking brings me up and I settle back on my knees. Then I take my yellow cap, dip it into the water, and pour it over my head. The cold washes down my face and soaks my back and chest. It feels so good. I fill it many times to pour it over my head, and when I fill the cap one last time, I put it back on my head and leave it there dripping.

When I lie back in the grass, it receives my worn body in the softest of beds. The wet cap covers my closed eyes, and the white end of a grass stem slips between my lips. It tastes sweet. Bees play light music in the gentle breeze of the meadow. When I wake, the sun has disappeared behind the peaks. Time to get going down to the dirt road, and then a slow, stiff walk to the car. I look all around me, one last time, at this beauty, this life that touches the deepest part of me with peace.

But this was a dream about a glorious day on Mt. Yale. Now I wake. I find myself in the dreadful predicament I was in before the dream gave me its comforting respite.

CHAPTER 8

AWAKENING

I roll onto my side and stare dully at the edge of the shelf into the black water below. I know I must get up and go on, but where?

When I sit up, I see nearby a large fallen tree. From out of the surrounding darkness its white trunk beckons. For some reason, its light, round shape feels safe to me. I move toward it, stepping on fallen branches, escaping from the dark pool. As it has been many times before and will be all through these hours, there are no thoughts about the past few minutes. The plan to continue down the creek to a highway vanishes. To this day, I'm struck by how many times I would forget a thought or a place within minutes of encountering a new thought and place. Walking beside the luminous tree, I grasp hold of its dead limbs to steady myself. At the end of the fallen tree the level ground changes. A hill rises so steeply that it makes walking impossible. Down on all fours, I crawl. How far to the top? When I look up, I see two shadowy figures along the top of the hill. I don't know what they are. They're giants. A pang of fear hits, but still, I struggle toward them. What else can I do? I continue to dig my hands in the mud and push my feet to where the giants are because I'm sure that when I get there, the way to the parking lot will clear. This is the first I've thought about the parking lot for hours.

The slope slides me backward. Oblivious to the pain, I grab at tree limbs, thorn plants, and muddy rocks trying to pull myself up.

When the angle of the slope eases, the silhouetted giants that frightened me at the start have become trees.

Instead of discovering the car a short distance away, I fall again and roll down into another, steeper gully. I kick my heels in to stop and lie breathless. There is no strength in me to turn around and go back up to the ridge where I stood only moments ago. All the effort of getting out of the pool and crawling up the steep hill makes continuing down this other side the only choice I can make. I stand and sidestep. The rain slows, and a mist takes its place. All at once, I bump into a log. What I can see of it looks much larger than the one by the pool of water, and it feels rough with bark. Then my feet slide under it, and I struggle to stand, grasping the trunk with both arms. I can see nothing above or below me, nor can I make out one end of the log or the other. When I'm somewhat stable, I run my hands both ways on the top of the log, and it seems lower to my left.

With every new obstacle, there's a new idea to overcome it. Now at this giant log in the dark, I puzzle out that maybe this fallen tree forms a bridge over a gully I can't see. It could be deep and dangerous. This log can keep me from falling into it. If I can climb up on it and crawl to the upward end then I can slide off the other side. Maybe I can touch the ground on that side. It makes wearied sense to me. All my failed ideas make sense. There's a limb a foot or so on the side of the log, and I swing my right foot up on it and push, swinging my left leg over the trunk, trying to pull with my arms. I'm on top of the log. I shinny a few feet along, clinging to its enormous girth with both arms and legs wrapped around it. I'm terribly frightened. I could fall off this giant log into a dark, deep pit that I imagine is below me. For just a moment, that fear conjures up the fall I'd taken earlier into the nearly inescapable pool of water. I might fall here as I did there. I scoot forward a few feet, stop, and then scoot back. I'm worried that one or both ends of the dead tree end over a precipice. Clinging to the girth, I lay my cheek on the rough wood and fall asleep. When I awaken, the darkness hasn't changed. I close my eyes to sleep. It will be light when I wake, but I can't sleep.

Without consideration, I once again shinny forward until I come to the end of the log. Leaning over one side, I see the ground. At that moment, seeing the ground means nothing to me, yet it is the coming of dawn.

I must get off this large, dead log, so I pivot on my belly so that my feet are above the ground and let myself fall. Surprisingly, it is only a couple of feet to the ground. I lean against the log, move my left foot around in a half-circle, and then my right, to make sure the ground doesn't fall away. The ground is firm. The sky lightens, and I notice that the log bridges a gully that in one direction plunges steeply, and on the other, it's a mild slope. Somehow, I got off on the gentle side.

Go up. Going up means I'll find a place to look out a long way, and I'll be able to find out where I am. I know I will be able to look down at the parking lot. I wonder if I still have the car keys. I reach into one back pocket and the other in a panic. I have to have the keys to start the car, to get home. Both back pockets are empty. I stuff my hands into the front pockets. In the left one, I feel the outline of the keys and the warmth of the metal close to my body. Now I know I'll make it.

I trudge upward as the sky lightens, giving the trees a shape above me, and the line of a hilltop. With fits and starts, I make my way up to the ridge. I notice that something is in my mouth. It feels stuffed with fuzzy cotton, but also hard. I pay it no mind. The hill doesn't end on a high place where I can look out, but in a semi-circle of near vertical rock with boulders beneath it. Stepping closer, I reach out and touch the wall, looking for a way to climb up. This habit of finding a route up a rock is an old one, but it is impossible because I can hardly walk.

Backing away from the wall, I look toward the strengthening light. The ground looks level that way. Pine trees stand along the way with a passable distance between them. This is the way to go. I can only shuffle, weaving like a drunk. The slope has a gentle rise now, but I cannot catch my breath. Often sinking to my knees to breathe, I feel I can't go on, that I can't get to where I'm going. But, of course, I don't know where I'm going. Then I'm on the ground. I've run into a tree trunk and slumped down with blood on my forehead. I fall more than once and this violence scratches my face with the rough bark.

My desire for water is intense. Swallowing rasps down my throat with pain, and that wad of something inside my mouth feels fat and aches. I sit up and lean against a tree trunk. Why am I so out of breath just sitting here? My lips sting when I touch them, but they are not lips, but a thick bulge of scabs. Pine needles drip with the all-night rain. The ground is squishy. But for me this place, in all its wetness, is a desert---directionless.

I grasp at the low limbs to stand, then lean against the bark. When I do, I think, go toward the sunrise. That's all. The forest thickens when the ground tilts downward. I weave ahead with eyes down, chin to my chest until something barely catches my eye. A flicker of color. I stop in front of a thick wire strung between two trees waist high like a place horses could be tied. For a second time my eye catches the flicker of red above me. One of the tree branches has a faded red ribbon tied to it. It flutters in the gentle breeze. I know what it is! Ribbons like this mark a trail. When a trail is sketchy from little use, or in winter when it's covered in snow, the markers help hikers keep on the path. Why is this one here? I walk around the tree in circles, staring down at the ground to find the trail, but there is no sign of one. I sit down hard, bowing my head between my legs. There's a ribbon. Hope stirs from a wire and a faded red ribbon.

I lower my gaze down into the small valley. At the bottom, a brook runs in a place full of sunshine. It fills a small pond sur-rounded by green plants flourishing in warmth. After taking two awkward steps down, I slip and fall on my face. As I struggle to get up. I notice movement above the small valley on the hill opposite from me. The hill rises almost straight up, and covered with boulders the size of cars. In the midst of them, there are moving shapes. At first, I can't tell what they are. They are people. People wearing shorts and T-shirts with backpacks strapped on their backs. They must be hiking on a trail through those boulders. I yell at them, but they keep hiking up the trail. Later, in the hospital, I come to understand that I experienced many hallucinations.

I kneel to call out again. They don't turn, so I try to hurry down the hill to get closer to call out to them. When I reach the brook, it's wider than I thought and maybe deeper. I fear water. Deep water. Two dead trees have been placed over a narrow place where the brook enters the pond. I take slow and careful steps, but even with this caution, I slip and fall into the shallow water. I bang my knee against stones on the bottom of the pond.

I don't remember the fall I had last night into the water. Yet, an overwhelming anxiety churns inside me after having slipped into this shallow pool and banging my knee. I splash across the few steps left in the water and hang my head coughing. When I look up, I see the grasses grow high, and sand borders the pool on this side of it. I am so thirsty.

I lie on my belly on what looks like a miniature beach and dip my head down into the water, immersing my ears and drinking until choking pulls me up. I lift my head out of the water coughing and plunge my head again and again deep into this life-saving drink. When I can drink no more, I lay back in the softness of the grass and turn my head to see the surprise of yellow flowers dotting the green. A sweet smell surrounds me like the smell of cucumbers or watermelon. All of this, the water, the warmth of the sun, the sand, the grasses, and flowers, I take in. I close my eyes and sleep. When I wake, I crawl over and slide on my belly into the shallow water, stretch my head to a deeper part and dip in to drink my fill again.

CHAPTER 9

REVIVAL

AFTER this respite, I think about the hikers I saw through the boulders on the meandering trail, striving to get to the top of the rock-strewn ridge. Hope comes again after water and rest. I must follow them. I get up and begin to climb boulder after boulder, crawling over and between them desperately trying to reach the trail they were on. The slope grows steeper and the boulders larger. More and more I struggle. Breathing deeply brings a searing pain in my chest, and the aching thirst begins again. My effort to climb quicker fails me as I stop every few moments panting, both hands gripping a rock as big as a car. Where are the people? I know I saw them, but I'm only a short way up the rise.

I attempt to climb over the next boulder and struggle to get on top of it. When I do, I slump on my stomach with my hands holding on to both sides. My fear returns. The huge rocks lie toppled on each other without end. They've grown bigger. I can go no farther. Looking back, I see the safe place of the pool of water below where the sun warms the soft grass, the sand, and most of all, water. I turn around.

When I get back to safety and sit, my feet ache, and I take off my boots. My socks are too hard to pull off, so I soak my socks and feet in the cold water until they tingle with the cold. The numbing is welcome. I pivot onto my belly again and dip my head to try to satisfy this thirst that doesn't end. When I turn to sit, I suddenly catch movement. Up the small valley where the brook comes to me, there is something or somebody. I shade my eyes to see.

Maybe forty or fifty yards away on the left bank, people stand under the canopy of a tree. It's a man standing beside two women. Their backs are toward me. The man is small and has a black bowler hat on his head. He's holding an open black umbrella over the heads of his companions. No one is moving. They seem to be concentrating on something. I cry out to them with a voice stronger than before the water. They don't turn. Clearing my voice, I yell to them many times, "I'm here! Look! Help." I get up and try to run, but can only walk. I cross back over the brook on the tall, water-logged trees, continuing to call as I go. My voice goes unnoticed. Maybe they are walking on a path that is above this small stream. Maybe it goes into the forest ahead of them. I have to get up the embankment alongside the water, and walk to the tree that they stood under. I have to find the path I know they are walking on. But, when I get there, no one is there, and there is no path. They've moved on. I yell out once more, but, again, there is no answer. Still, I feel hope. The three of them were standing right on this spot. It's just that they didn't hear me. I'll catch up with them soon. Because there is no trail, I decide that they are walking alongside the stream. I'm sure of it.

The sound of the water intensifies as the slope steepens and slows me. No matter, I'm convinced that they are just ahead. Suddenly, my head swims with dizziness, and I slip to my knees, and with my forehead in the dirt between my legs, I cry out to them. When I'm able to get up, I move toward the top of a knoll where the stream divides. One part goes into a heavily wooded forest, the other runs into an open place. Not a soul in sight.

I imagine that they took the left fork of the stream, and went into the shade of the forest where it's cool, cooler than it is here. Only a little while ago, I drank and rested, but I am thirsty again. I don't drink. All I care about now is to find out where the man and his two companions went. I take a few steps and then stop to look around. On my right, a hill rises with trees spread far apart. Without a reason why, I begin to slog up the hill on the other side of the stream. Near the top of the hill is a rickety, weatherworn fence. In some places it stands, in others it lies on the ground. Beyond the fence the trees end, and then it is flat and wide. On the far side of it, I see a broad grassy valley. It's lovely. Safe. I should go down into this calm welcoming place. I walk back and forth along the fence until I find a place where three rusty barbed wire strands have fallen to the ground. I decide I should step over and walk on the level ground to look down into the valley.

Now I think of the three people I tried to catch up with who may have gone a different way. Maybe they didn't go into the forest at all, but through a fringe of trees, and then up and over into the valley before me. Maybe I can see their trail alongside the valley from this hill I'm on. I stand still in the silence and to decide about where to go next.

I feel that all of this place, the fence, the water, and the valley, must be part of a large farm. The fence is an animal enclosure. I'll find the farmhouse. I step over the wire and walk out into the sunshine, wondering how to get down into the valley. I need to reach the farmhouse, but I don't move. I'm fearful about moving away from the fence and not being able to find my way back to it and my small pool of water, sand, and pillow grass. I decide to walk straight out from the fence, so if I need to come back, I can turn around and go straight back.

When I walk out from the fence, the view opens up to hills of various heights, and gullies running with water. Precipitous rock outcroppings jut up from the sides of various washes and the broad stream. How beautiful it all is! Many shades of green under sunlight. Pastoral. My emotions flip from fear to peace. Down into those warm grassy places, I'll be safe.

I'm suddenly terrified. Something's wrong. The valley and the broad meadow are too big, too green. Nothing looks like this on Haleakala. Haleakala is dry, mostly barren.

Fear of the valley turns me back to the fence. I step over the strands of rusty wire lying on the ground. I want to go back to the stream, back to the pool to drink and rest. I see in my mind the tree bridge over the creek and the pool. Oh yes, the pool of cold water with its sandy shore and the tall, soft grass. I no longer think of the man with the umbrella and his lady friends. I stumble back down to the stream, and then along it to the pond. I lay myself down on my belly and dip my head into the water.

No matter how much I drink, I can't get enough. The thirst diminishes for only a short time, and then it returns with the same intense longing. I don't want to leave this place, but I stand anyway, cross the water, and struggle back up the hill where the red ribbon fluttered on the limb. It's hot. I'm empty.

The wire droops when I hold it with both hands. I try to reach for the tree limb where the ribbon hangs limp. It's too high. I don't know why I want to touch it. Roaming around the ribboned tree, I search for another red marker. Out of the corner of my eye, I see one hanging from a branch. I walk down to it in thick mud where the sun has not warmed the ground; I see a boot print impressed in the mud, and next to it, a smaller print barely shows. This one has a square impression on the arch, like a label. I can't read it. Maybe these boot prints tell me that there's a trail here. I walk down further and see the same large boot print, and next to it, the smaller one. Then there are more ribbons in the trees. It's a trail!

Sweat stings my eyes with the heat from the sun now overhead. The yellow cap would have helped to keep the sweat out of my eyes, but I don't remember the cap. Even though it's hot, the warmth comforts me and feels good on my neck. My soaked, mud-clotted cotton pants begin to dry out. I look at my white pants; they are no longer white. The footprints that were distinct before begin to fade in what have become two tracks of a rough gravel road. Further down, a trail splits off from it on the left side. I look at the rough tracks, and then at trail. Confused. Should I continue down, or go up the trail?

I turn up the trail. Soon, out of breath, I have to stop. Here the path makes a steep switchback, and, in the distance, another one. I turn back to the road and its welcome downward slant. But when I reach it, I stop again, full of anxiety. This road must go down into Haleakala's crater. I'm certain that large trucks go up and down here with water for the cabins. I suppose only the rangers know about this road. It goes way, way down there. "Don't go down," my mind warns. Better to climb back up to the trail. It leads to the parking lot. I hadn't thought of the parking lot for a while. Now, I believe that I'm near my waiting car, soon to be on my way home. I don't remember that there are no roads into the crater.

The sun beats down on me hard. Sweat rolls down my back and chest and even streams down my legs. The switchbacks end, and the path levels off so that it is possible to contour along the side of this huge slope that I can neither see the top of, nor the bottom. Repeatedly, the path weaves along the slope and often turns into shaded water-filled gullies, and then back out into the sun. Insects buzz about. There are moments of encouragement at seeing grass and flowers. Thirst is my constant companion. Why I don't stop to drink is a puzzle. Maybe fear of slipping on the rocks in the water and not being able to get up. Maybe it is the old mantra of not wanting to stop, wanting to push on, wanting to reach the goal. So I don't drink any water.

The trudging is endless. My head rests against my chest, eyes focused on the ground to avoid banging my feet against a rock, or sliding out-of-control down a drenched slope. I look up now and then, and then back to my steps. Once, when I look up, I stop because there are three giant slabs of rock that tower over me, and then they plunge down into the abyss. I am quite certain that these towering slabs end at the bottom of the crater where there is a cabin. That's where the rangers are. That's where they are right now. They have water and food.

It's clear to me that all I need to do is keep going around this mountainside, splashing through all these gullies until I get to the side of that first cliff, and then go straight down to the rangers. I pick up my pace. I stare at the knife-edged rock walls. When I'm close to them, I can't go on because they stand wickedly high, smooth, and nearly straight up and down. Looking down at the edge of this first one, I can't see the end, the crater, or a cabin. I can't go down there.

Immediately, a new idea pops into my head: keep on this trail because it leads to the top of this giant hillside. Then I will go down the other side of this mountain, or hill, whatever it is. Down is best. Why it's best I don't know. It just is. The path doesn't lead to the top of anything, but to a saddle between the rock slabs on my right and the summit of the giant hill that I can't see on my left. The trail I've been following crosses the saddle and then goes down into a deep forest. I feel the coolness. Out of the heat on one side and into the cool and mud of this side. In the mud, I see the same footprints that I saw before. I get down on my knees to look more closely. They are the same. One is larger than the other, and the small one has a square mark in the center of the sole. I touch them, moving my fingers around their impressions in the mud. I'm on the right trail. I'm sure of it, and sure that the parking lot is not far away. Through the pains in my body, the hunger, and the thirst, some hope raises me to my feet. I cannot be far now.

I breathe in the fresh smell of damp ground and rotting leaves— so different from the steaming plants on the hot side of the climb up to here. Soon enough, I change. The pleasantness of the new smells wears off, and the despair returns. I wonder if this forest path ever ends. I've been walking for hours. My desires vacillate between water and the car in the lot. Those thoughts are punctuated by the pain of the lump inside my mouth. I'm walking numb until I hear a familiar sound. Water. Running water.

A sharp corner on the pathway opens into a wide stream, cascading over shelves of flat rocks. Sinking my head into this stream is my only goal. I hesitate. The water rushes fast here and deep with no place to cross. Below me, the steepness flattens, becoming shallow on the far side. I can drink over there. I'm standing on a steep hill next to the rushing water. I know I can't cross here because I'm certain I'd fall and be hurled into the stream and over a waterfall. But, getting down from here to where the water flattens, and I can cross to the other side, will be very difficult. I'm frightened. I don't know what to do.

I sit down next to the fast running stream on a steep bank of sloppy mud. It would be easy to topple into them. Time passes, I need water. My fingers dig deep into the mud. When I scoot down a few inches at a time the spray soaks me. I can only slide down little by little. Even with hands and heels pressing into the mud, I slide out of control. Suddenly, the toes of my boots strike a large rock sticking out of the mud that rolls me on my belly headfirst, and then I stop. I don't move for a while, and finally, roll over on my back, looking up at the sky. It is a long time before I can catch my breath. When I do, I discover I'm only a few feet from the shallow part of the stream where it may be possible to cross to drink.

When I stand, my clothes, my hair, everything is soaked with mud. After a few steps, I slip on a submerged flat rock and fall hard on my butt. I get to my knees and put my hand in the water to push up to stand, but dizziness and nausea come in waves. I put my head down between my legs. No thought of drinking now. Vertigo slows so that I can stand and begin to walk hesitantly to the other bank. When I get there, I collapse face down on the ground next to the stream. I'm drowsy. I wait to drink because it's hard to swallow. After a rest, I drink a little at a time. I get to my knees, and then sit back on my butt in the shallow water.

CHAPTER 10

Hallucinations

DOWN the river where I look, a fence crosses it with its posts high in the air above the rushing water. It's too steep to go there, and the forest thickens below. To the right of me, I see another fence, a different fence going up a bare hill with only brush and wild grasses. It must lead somewhere, so I decide to follow it. I must move carefully because the plants and wild grasses are soaked from the storm last night, and they are slick. I'm too exhausted to walk, and my legs are heavy from fatigue. It feels like hours of crawling to get to the fence. I plan to pull myself up on a post and then go hand over hand on the wires attached to the other posts. The hill is so steep I may not be able to stand and walk and may only be able to crawl. When I pull on a post to stand, I tip sideways into the slick swale. Once again, sleep takes me away.

I rouse myself to get up to pee. Until now, I've stood, undone my pants, and relieved myself. I can't do that anymore because I can't unzip my filthy pants, so I pee in them. It feels good, not only to relieve myself but for the unexpected warmth it provides. From now on, I take many opportunities to warm myself in this way.

I start crawling up post-by-post, pulling with both hands around the bottom of each, and pushing with my knees. I reach the top of the hill and see another one ahead. I get to my knees and then stand leaning against a tree. There's a shallow valley between where I am and the top of the next hill.

There is something very different over there. A man is looking at me, and a woman stands beside him, and next to her is a large green tent. The man leans down to fuss with a tent peg, driving it into the ground with a rock. The woman smiles at a little girl who is playing in front of the tent in a blue plastic wading pool, splashing water in all directions with her feet. The girl reaches over the side of the pool to pick up a plastic beach ball and giggles, as she throws it at her mother.

I yell to them, "Hi! Hi! Over here!" I wave both arms over my head and shout again, "Please don't go away! I'll be right over." The woman waves to me; the man motions for me to come over to them while the little girl jumps out of the pool, giggles again, and goes into the tent. It takes a long time for me to slide down the hill on my side and then climb up to them. It's like a jungle down at the bottom with thick undergrowth that keeps me struggling flat on my belly. At the bottom is a small brook. I don't stop to drink because I must get up to the family as fast as I can. They will have something for me to eat and drink. The slope upward is very steep with nothing to pull me along. Soon, I turn over on my side and once again thrash uphill. I keep my mind focused on the place where a welcoming family waits for me. They will have water and maybe warm clothes.

I'm afraid they will forget about me and disappear; that fear keeps me moving. Little by aching little, I struggle upward until I stand on top of the hill where they wait, but as I look around, I don't see anyone. The top is empty except for a few trees with flickering light between their leaves. Ahead is a short rise. They must be on that one. Walking a few minutes in that direction, I call out, "Hey, I'm here. Do you see me? I'm right here!" I wave my hands and pee for the warmth as I wave.

It strikes me that maybe they didn't see or hear me, even though they waved. It must have taken me longer than I realized to get over here. They've left for their car. Just to make sure, I walk down a little, and then up a little, hoping to see the tent. There is no tent. There is no family. I walk in widening circles, searching for them, but there is no one here and no sign of a tent. I catch sight of something blue on a tree limb, a ribbon waving. Beneath it runs a faint trail. It goes somewhere. From that moment on, I never give another thought to the family. I'm convinced that this sketchy path leads to the parking lot and my car.

The path leaves the soggy forest and leads to a dry, open place. It contours around several bare hills when, unexpectedly, beside the path, runs a fence. I don't understand these fences. Some are broken and others stand tall and straight. There is hope in the fences. The trail goes alongside it, and I continue. The air feels cooler, and the sun isn't overhead, but slants. It might be late. It might get dark soon. Deep inside, I know I can't stay in this place at night. There is a dim sense about last night's ordeal. Even if it's getting late, I know the parking lot is very close. On my left stand a few scraggly bushes. Long dry slices in the ground show where the rain has come down. To the right, down the slope, are pine trees, and then, in an opening through the trees, something moves. I decide to leave the trail and go down to the window-like opening in the forest.

Something moves again. I scoot down one of the ravines. It soon deepens into dark shadows. I crawl back up and go down the other ravine. It is easier. When I reach the edge of the trees they are dense, blocking my view. I move my head side-to-side and the opening in the trees appears and grows wider. Through this window, I stare at black asphalt. Along its edge, to the right, stands a large wooden sign. I recognize it at once because I've walked from my car to this sign many times. A map of the trail is on it, along with photos and explanations of the plants and wildlife along the Halemau'u trail. In front of the sign, stand a man and a woman looking at the map. The woman turns to her companion and says something. He looks back at her and smiles. They wear colorful jackets with the hoods down. His is orange like my worthless windbreaker and hers, green. They must be rainproof and breathable. Their packs are first class, no doubt stuffed to the brim with all that they will ever need for safety and comfort on their hike. They both wear new hiking boots, wool socks, and gaiters that tell me they know what they are doing.

I look up and turn my attention toward the top of the lot. Two parked cars sit there with each of the front tires pushed against the logs to keep them from tipping down the mountain. Neither looks like my old Toyota. It must be out of view at the far end of the lot beside the port-a-potty. I look back at the hikers, cup my hands around my mouth, and give a loud call. They don't look up. They concentrate on the map and the notices that say, "No Camping in the Crater." "No Feeding Animals or Birds." "Pack Out Your Trash." I call out several more times, but with no response. My hope sinks.

I have to get to hikers before they set off. Right there, right in front of me, is the parking lot. People. Cars. But I'm suddenly paralyzed with fear, afraid to go through these trees. They are dusky and frighteningly closed in. There must be another way to get there. I scramble back up the ravine to a flat place where yet another fence sticks up that I hadn't seen when I went down the ravine. I walk the fence line in one direction for a time, and then back to where I started and beyond. I must find a way down to the people, to my car. The black asphalt must be warm, and the people would help me, but I can't get there.

It doesn't register to me that every person I see disappears. I don't remember seeing anyone. There is only this moment. I don't recall the crater trail, the fierce storm, the injuries, not even the misery of pain and cold. I've already forgotten the people I'd just seen at the trailhead parking lot. Each moment is my only awareness. The drive inside me is to get out of here, to get safe.

The sun catches my attention. It's about to slip behind the trees at the top of a long, steep hill above this barren place where I stand. I'm shivering. I decide to go up there, to the trees and away from this barren place. I'm compelled to go up into the trees because I believe it is warm among them. I look up at them and feel the steepness, but I must go up to the warmth.

The dark comes quickly, and soon I can barely see where I'm going. I feel the dirt underneath my feet and avoid openings of ruts and deeper holes. I have to crawl again on my knees or scoot on my chest over mounds of dirt. There is a feeling of dread about this place. I push hard to escape from this deeply fractured ground that surrounds me. My hands continually scrape against the rocks. I stand up and look around. I take a tentative step and then, immediately, stumble headlong into a dark hole. My head slides along a cold wall of dirt. I push and pull with my hands to get out. When I do escape, I lie stiffly, paralyzed by fear.

I roll over on my back, looking up at the endless dark mountain ahead of me. When I lay back, I think of Ron my pal of more than fifty years. We've climbed many mountains together and solved some of the problems they gave us, or, at other times, we've had to turn back. A problem might be how to climb up through a difficult pitch on a rock face, or where to descend a couloir filled with snow. Should we take plunge steps in the soft snow warmed by the sun, or use our ice-axes to climb down backwards down snow hardened solid by the cold shade? We escaped from lightning storms and walked down endless trails in the dark after a day of climbing. If he were here, in this awful place, we'd figure a way out together. Slowly, I remember the most dangerous experience that Ron and I had on a mountain.

We are both exhausted after several strenuous hours of climbing long pitches on a peak, and neither of us has any certainty about how many more until we reach the top. He yells up at me when he's ready to climb, "Climbing." I confirm with "Climb," as he begins up the nearly vertical face. It is a long distance between us on this wall. We are tied together by a hundred and fifty feet of rope if we need it. I sit above on small ledge with a thick waistband of blue nylon tied around me. I'm anchored to the rock above me by a sling clipped to the waistband and then fastened to a metal blade driven solidly into a crack to protect us in case of a fall. Ron begins to climb up to where I am. I pull the rope up when there is slack that would be dangerous for him in case of a fall, but I give him slack to maneuver when rope is too tight.

I haven't seen him for several minutes because where I'm sitting is not as steep as where he's climbing, so there's a lip of rock blocking my view. His knit cap comes into view below me, but not straight below. Just as I had, Ron too has moved to his right several feet to get around a difficult place, so that now the rope is at an angle between us, which means there would be slack between us if he fell. If he fell it would be a free fall until gravity put him in a straight line beneath me. That could be disastrous for both of us because of the increased weight of his body falling free. Though tired we're doing well. We've made other climbs like this.

I keep focused on his knit cap until it vanishes. There is a brief moment before the rope accelerates on my left palm, the braking hand, burning deeply with falling weight. The fall seems like forever and like an instant. The rope slows with the braking and then stops. My buddy is swinging in the air tied to the end of the rope. I hold him with the rope right around my back and in my hand. I, too, am dangling in the air between the sling attached to me and the piton on the other end. There is only silence.

I yell down, "You okay?"

He calls back in a voice pinched by the strain of the rope tight around his waist, "Yeah," and adds, "I can't stay here. I'm in the air. You have to pull me up."

I holler back, "Is there a ledge?"

"Yeah," he answers as he moves to the ledge.

I continue to hold on, but I don't know how long I can. Then the rope around me slackens.

He calls up, "I'm on the ledge."

We're safe for the moment. I turn my palm over to see what damage happened to my bare hand as the rope ripped through it. I expect to see blood, but there is only a deep groove in the skin. The speed of the rope has cauterized my palm. We talk back and forth, trying to decide what to do. Should we go up to the top or rappel down to the ground at the base of the cliff far below? We are many rope lengths above the ground and maybe going to the top might mean finding another, easier way down. When I turn and look up, I can't see the top. The sun is low. We are both trembling. We're both badly shaken and completely exhausted. We agree it is best to go down.

We rappel down the rope many times, protected by pitons and slings anchored in the cracks of the wall. The sun is gone behind the mountain now. The only light is from the alpenglow on the peaks that surround us. The glow cheers us for the short time it lasts. At last, we stand in the dark on the ground. We drink the dregs from our water bottles. We have nothing to eat, as we start down the trail with our arms around each other's shoulders beneath the rising of a full moon.

CHAPTER 11

FLATIRONS

THE memory of the two pals finding their way down and out of danger fades, but leaves me feeling encouraged. As before, I roll onto my hands and knees and continue crawling through the dirt mounds and the pits between them. Everything that surrounds me hides in the darkness, except for the silhouette I see above me at the top of the long hill. I stand, putting my head down to clear the dizziness. I take a few tentative steps, stop, and look up again. I can hardly believe what I am seeing. I make out several slabs of rock jutting into the sky. They are exactly like the Flatirons above Boulder. I'm sure that's what they are, flat slabs of rock tilted upward. They must be warm from the sun beating on them all day. I shudder from the cold, but there is also the comfort from the thought that when I get up to the top, I will lie down on them and bask in their warmth. Then when I awake in the morning, the sun will warm me further. It's the warmth I crave and sleep. Sleep is a healer. I have a notion that from there I'll see lights—the glow of Kahului and Wailuku down by the ocean.

I begin to climb up into the gully that will end at the Flatirons, but immediately I know it will be a great struggle, maybe impossible. I only manage a step or two on the steep sand and small rocks, and then slip backward, sometimes losing what I had gained. The angle of the slope increases, and I must stop to breathe every few steps.

After a while I can only crawl, gripping deep into the sand to pull myself up a little at a time. It is all I can manage.

When I rest, a voice inside me tells me to keep going. My eyes are closed all the time now, but my mind sees the lights on people's porches in the towns below. I imagine the Denny's restaurant in Kahalui where I can fill my belly with pancakes. But the sharp pains in my fingers, as they dig into the rocks and dirt, shake me out this reverie. When I try to stand, inevitably I fall on my face and begin crawling again. I know it's better to crawl to gain one foot at a time, but I want to stand and walk, thinking it will be easier and quicker to reach those slabs up there. It isn't easier.

My entire world diminishes into brief chunks of moments in the relentless drive to get out of wherever I am and to the car, to get home. I'm not thinking about dying and have little awareness of the brutal beating my body is taking, or the events of the preceding hours. For an instant, I'm struck with a profound sense of remorse. I want to tell my wife how sorry I am to worry her, but at the moment I feel sure I can get out of here and back home before too long.

I keep crawling and slipping for an endless time until I look up and find myself at the foot of the warm slabs of the sandstone Flatirons. Relief pours over me as I gaze at them. Then, they seem to move. I feel dizzy and bend down to clear my mind. I look up again. The longer I look, the more these huge flat rocks seem to be moving in the light breeze, which makes me shiver. I wrap my arms around myself and shake my head to focus my eyes, but I can't stop the rocks from swaying. They seem to sway back and forth like trees, and then I realize they are trees silhouetted against the light of a starry sky. I collapse to my knees with my forehead in the dirt and weep without tears.

This is not the Haleakala I know. I don't know where I am, but I'm not there, not with all these tall trees above me. They don't grow in the crater or on the arid side where the highway goes to the summit. I am lost, so very, very lost. I can't fathom my weariness, but keep moving because this is all I can do. I tremble again and again as the night chill rolls over me. No Flatirons offer me the day's heat to rest, and sleep. All I want now is to get out of this horrible place. I scream, "I hate these trees." "I hate you, you lying, damn trees." I walk sideways along the hill beneath them. It's the only way I can walk. Whatever strength remains will not carry me up or down, so I stumble along the side of this steep slope. Soon, I'm walking on level ground with an embankment on both sides. My boots slip and slide in mud, and when I look down I see a slim glimmer of water. I can't walk anymore. I sink down to drink, but the water is only inches deep. For a time my unquenchable thirst was forgotten in the struggle up the Flatirons, now it returns. But I can only catch a tiny bit of water by sluicing it through my teeth to keep out the grit. There is not much to drink. All I want is sleep.

I stand and lean against one side of the gully that is over my head. I know I must not fall asleep. If I sleep, I won't wake up. I'll die here. My family and friends would be devastated. I must get home. With these thoughts, I urge myself to stay awake. If I stand, I'll stay awake and won't die. I figure that if I cross my arms and put my hands in my armpits to keep them warm, the warmth will keep me awake. I stare at the black form of the bank across from me to keep my eyes open. I watch the trees flutter in the breeze.

Later the moon rises above the trees on my left side. Seeing it rouses me to the idea that if I watch the moon all through the night until dawn, I will have made it. I will have stayed alive. So, I watch the moon.

I startle awake in a pale light. My mind is blank. What happened? I've slipped from standing against the gully bank to lying on the ground with my boots in the sludge. I look around and over my right shoulder see the moon going down. On my right shoulder? The moon is to the right when it was to the left. I fell asleep sometime in the night. But I'm alive.

My pants are soaked with urine. I try to sit up. I can't. I try again, but only flounder on my back. Then I lie still and then worry the bleeding sores on my cracked lips. When I swallow, it feels like there's a stone in my mouth, maybe covered with something fuzzy, and my tongue is numb. I must drink. I roll over onto my chest in the damp mud and struggle to my hands and knees. Leaning into the small run of water, my lips touch the surface and try to suck it, but there is more grit than liquid. I lie down and push the toes of my boots in the wet sand to create a little dam. Trickle by trickle, the water fills in behind the dam. I wait to let some of the grit settle and suck in whatever water I can. There is less than a mouthful of water. Every now and then the excruciating pain in my mouth flares up, and with that the tears run down my cheeks. I have to swallow around something.

I must get up. I put my hands in the mud underneath my knees and push and try to stand, but I cannot move. I have only strength enough to stay on my hands and knees and push. I fall on my belly after each try. I know that I will die here. I can't get up because I have nothing left but weariness and pain. I'm not afraid to die. Can't try any more. A vague peace covers me like a blanket. Simply wait.

CHAPTER 12

Up from the Mud

ON all fours, I wait. Suddenly, my hands feel a chill of water trickling beneath me. The cold stings my cut and bruised hands, and from somewhere, some strength comes to me. I push up and lean back on my boots to try to stand. I fall flat on my belly, gasping for breath, and try again. This time I push with my hands and arms as hard as I can, and finally I am standing—then bending over retching. Straightening up, I look up at the bank of the gully where I'd tried to stay awake, and it looks straight up and covered with dirt. I stand motionless, only gazing. I see a flicker. At the top of the embankment, a blue ribbon is tied to a tree branch. My hope is tenuous but alive. The blue ribbon means something.

I have to get up to that ribbon. I dig my fingers into the dirt and try to kick my toes into it. I grab and punch into the bank again and again until I am leaning against a leafless tree with a blue ribbon hanging above me. Tears roll down my cheeks and into my mouth. Trees cover the sky. When I look down, I see the tamping of a vague trail. I begin to walk again.

I take one long breath and walk slowly. I hum. Many years ago, I stumbled on to the idea that if I hummed a tune, I could keep an even pace hiking along a trail or climbing up a steep place off the trail. It might be a calypso song like Belafonte's, "Jamaica Farewell," or "Feeling Groovy," by Paul Simon. They served as a mantra, a calming with their steady routine. I don't know how this trick comes to me now, but it does and I hum.

The path skitters up and down, in and out of small gullies. Trees, bushes, and plants drip with moisture. Now and then, the trail vanishes into the underbrush. Each time it does, I'm afraid of losing my way. The thought of giving up is gone. Gone is the conviction that I am dying. I'm aware that I'm on a trail, that it is getting hot, and that I am sweating. For now, I've even forgotten about hunger and thirst. My focus is on walking. The possibility of losing the trail consumes me. I have to guess where the path will appear when it vanishes in front of my feet. When it disappears, I stop and turn in a circle, taking a step in each direction. Often, I see where it returns. When I don't, I just guess and start walking, and luckily the trail returns.

The humming stops as the trail that has been mostly level, now turns up at a sharp angle. My steps slow considerably; my breathing is shallow. Still, somehow, I move up this hellish mountain of a hill. The sun glares overhead through the trees. The heat becomes intense, creating a stifling, humid odor from dampness covering all the green. The sun must be high. I just keep moving.

Rounding one of the sharp bends on the pathway, a space opens across a large gully. I stop to look at something on the edge of the forest on the other side of the openness. A car sits there. It's an old Ford convertible. It is a red, 1949 two-door Ford convertible with its black top down. It has shiny chrome bumpers and hubcaps with white-wall tires. This is exactly the first car I owned when I was a 16-years old. Tendrils of plants grow out from the open trunk and the edges of the hood and cover the seat. This bright sparkling car is a sign. It tells me that I'm on the way to the parking lot. The parking lot had been long forgotten, and I think of it again. I move further along the path that weaves its way nearer to the fancy old red convertible until it vanishes.

Soon before me is a small grassy meadow with a mother and her young daughter sitting on a gingham blanket, reaching in and taking food from a picnic basket. The mother retrieves chicken legs and thighs wrapped in waxed paper. They drink Coca-Cola from glass bottles. The mother wears a breezy white dress with a pale pink ribbon around her waist. Her feet are bare. The little girl sits cross-legged in a blue dirndl with bright yellow straps. Maybe the mom and the little girl aren't real. I can't tell. I decide not to look at them anymore.

I hear a whirring sound above the canopy of trees. It startles me out of my trudging stupor. The noise grows louder, and through a slight break in the trees' canopy, I momentarily see a black helicopter. Then I can't see it but still hear it. The sound fades and returns three more times. They're looking for me. Before the last pass, I pull off my t-shirt and wave it back and forth, but the trees are thick and the engine fades away. I feel a mixture of hope and despair. The forest stills, but for birdsong.

I walk like a drunk. Shadows are moving to the other side of the trees. Days pass, months, and years until I'm surprised by another blue ribbon to keep me going. I know that I cannot stay alive another night. Even so, I feel no sadness. My feet are numb. I'm stooped by pains in my back.

The light-barked rainforest trees have turned dark and seem to be pines. The ground is dirt, not green with growing plants, and it has become level. The stifling heat has become cool like a Colorado forest. It's a dim place, strange. The pines are tall and widely spaced from each other. I notice that ribbons hang from many of them. They are not just red and blue, also but yellow, green, and orange. Stranger still, some trees have their bark scraped away into a white square. There are circles of different colors painted on the trees, and inside each circle is a number. No order in the numbers, but random like five, nine, twelve, three, and so on. I doubt any of this is real.

Wanting to know for sure, I walk to the closest tree and touch the yellow circle and the red number inside it. Smooth. I touch the dark area surrounding the circle and it is all rough like bark. It is bark and the circle has been carved away and painted and so was the number. It's all real. Someone did this. I go on to several other trees, and they are all like the first. It is a stand of trees with ribbons and numbers. I don't understand any of it. People did this. They may be close by. I take comfort in the reality of the trees and the people who carved them.

Winding around the numbered trees, I see several trails going in different directions. Some go down the other side that I came up. Others go further up from this place. Some are trampled with use; others can barely be detected. They all go somewhere. I'm dizzy and afraid of retching again, so I lie down on my back. I sleep. I don't know how long, but when I wake I can't move, or maybe I just don't want to move. Then I sit up. I sit dumbfounded and remember another time of not wanting to move. I was running a half-marathon from the base of Pike's Peak to the top. The steep climb and the altitude made it very difficult. Above timberline, I kept looking for the summit, but the trail kept winding without any inkling of the end. Soon I wasn't running, but moving at a slow jog. I wasn't sure I couldn't go any farther. I didn't want to take another step. Then I was at the top unable to take another step. Two people on either side of the trail there wrapped me in a blanket and put their arms around me. I couldn't stop weeping.

I whisper to myself, "Stand and lean against the tree." I get up to walk to each of the trails and go a short way along each one. Two go to the left, maybe three to the right, all going up except for one that goes down, which is the continuation of the trail I hiked up. The notion of the parking lot strikes me again, and it has to be down, I think, maybe because I can't climb up again. I start down a way, and the trail divides in two. One levels off to the left, and the other continues down. The level isn't a choice I can make. Level means up.

Soon the trail widens and my shoes slop in the mud. The trees above me have no needles. Their leaves knit at their tops. I'm in a different place again. I walk like a toddler, weaving, stumbling, tripping, and falling. The trail widens to two tracks that look like a road, maybe for a jeep. I can't look ahead much further than the ground in front of me. I stare blankly at the ground, and only sense the turns in the gravel tracks around small hills, and the ups and downs. No thoughts, only the reflex to keep moving. I keep at this numbly until I step on a twisted strand of rusted barbed wire. I look up at two rotted posts holding up a sign with no letters.

It can't be real. As before, I rub my hands across its surface and snag a splinter. It is wood. I walk around to the other side and find carved letters—something like, "Wai . . . ma . . . atur ... Pre . . .e." They make no sense to me but tell me that I am somewhere.

I continue down, but only stare at my feet. Rarely can I look up to take in what's around me. The two-track road has half-buried wood logs lying crossways. Sometimes they look like bars of metal. I don't know why they are here.

I slow until I break into a cough that stops me, and once again I'm down on all fours. It feels like I'm suffocating. When the gasping subsides, I stand and begin walking, but now the road is going up. Steeply up. Every four or five steps, I stop to catch my breath. I'm like climbers on Mt. Everest who count four or five steps, then lean over their ice axes desperate for oxygen before they can start again. The way is steep, and I don't count steps or how long I rest.

After one rest, I look up the road and see a teenage girl sitting in the grass looking at me. She's far away, but I can see her put the white end of a blade of grass between her teeth and chew. I fall to my side and I relieve myself, grateful for the renewed warmth. When I stand, I look for the girl. There she sits, and I think to myself that she is not real, but then she looks up at me, takes the blade from her mouth, and smiles. I don't understand how she could be sitting there looking at me and yet not be there. Maybe she can help me. As I walk closer to her, she seems to get farther away from me, and yet all the while, she doesn't seem to move at all. I draw closer and she disappears. I whisper, "Thanks for not being real."

CHAPTER 13

Caring Hands, Cheerful Voices

THERE'S a fence. No memory of fences, yet there is something familiar about this place. I've been here before, several times. My mind clears as I look around. It's a campground. I see two tents on the grass, a restroom, and close to it, a Volkswagen camper parked in a small lot by the restrooms. The side door is open, and a woman steps out of the camper. She doesn't see me and although she's within shouting distance, I don't call to her for help. I don't want to frighten her or to be a burden. Mostly I'm embarrassed about the condition I'm in and being so foolish to get myself lost.

I vaguely recall that there's a gate farther down along the fence. I could go through that gate, and that way I wouldn't bother anyone. I weave myself down the fence line and find the gate, but it's locked. I try to climb over it. My boots slip on the wire, and I slam to the ground. I know I need help. Then I go through the old routine—I roll onto my stomach, get to my hands and knees, and struggle to stand. I walk back to where I saw the camper lady. I move along the fence until the camper comes into view. The lady continues doing whatever she is doing. I grasp the top wire with both hands and cry out, "Hi. I don't want to frighten you," but my voice is dry and muffled. I try again, "I don't mean to bother you," but again, what comes out is a croaking whisper. With whatever I have left, I let loose, "I need help!"

She turns. I know I've made a mistake. I've frightened her. She takes steps toward the fence and stops. I try to say more, but I can't. She cries out, "You're him. You're him, aren't you? The one who's lost. The ranger told us about you. We all thought you died." I try to explain. I can't. I slip down the fence in a clump and ask, "Do you have any water?"

She calls to her husband inside the camper, "He's here! That guy who was lost is by the fence!" The man steps out, then turns and grabs a folding camp chair and a blanket. He calls to his wife to get water. He runs toward me. My head feels heavy. I put it down on my chest. Something bangs on the ground near me, a camp chair. The husband climbs over the fence and puts his hands under my arms to help me into the chair, then wraps the blanket around my shivering body. I watch as his wife fills a large container with water. He climbs back over the fence and runs to take the water jug from her hand. When he comes back to me he gently smiles, and sets the half-gallon jug of water on my lap. Though my fingers are torn and spotted with dry blood, I lift the water to my chapped lips and drink and drink more. Soon, other campers come to the fence. Because I continue to shiver, someone brings another blanket, and it is wrapped tightly around me. People ask questions. "What happened to you? How do you feel? Are you okay?" They tell me how glad they are to see me, that I made it out alive. Forgetful, I ask, "Where am I?" A bearded man answers, "You're at the Hosmer Grove campground right near the park entrance." The sun is low. It's colder. Someone wraps a sleeping bag around my shoulders. The water is gone and then it is refilled, and I drink long and hard. I pee in my pants, but I'm not ashamed because I can't control much of anything. A helicopter flies overhead, hovers, and then lands in a field. More and more people gather looking, talking to each other, and asking me more questions. I'm flooded with emotion.

A woman in uniform climbs over the fence with ease. She kneels beside me. I look at her. She smiles at me and holds my gaze in her dark eyes. Her fingers and thumb grip my wrist to take my pulse. I try to talk to her, but nothing comes out except tears. She puts her arm around my shoulders and holds me tight. I feel her warmth. She whispers in my ear, "You are safe now. You are going to be okay." She holds my hand in both of hers and I lean my head against her. She's the park ranger.

There are sirens and many people in uniforms. Several climb the fence. One man takes my pulse again, then places a stethoscope on my chest. He shines a penlight in my eyes. Red lights are flashing and someone behind me is on the radio telling the ambulance to back down on the grass. Red lights. It's all very confusing to me. Out of desperation I ask, "Where's the ranger?" Someone points to her standing behind the medical people.

A group of men uniformed in dark blue stand together. They smile at me, asking questions about what happened, how I got lost, and how I found my way to the campground. I try to answer, but not much comes out. When I'm silent, a tall mustached man in khakis tells me about the search for me. The morning after I'd gone missing, a ground search began with local volunteers, police, and park personnel. They hiked through the crater on the major trails, camped out, and continued the next day. He and several others were from a search and rescue unit stationed in Honolulu. Some joined the ground search using search and rescue dogs flown over to Maui from Oahu. One helicopter from the Maui airport and another over from Honolulu took many passes through the crater, the northeastern slopes, and across the rainforest over the last two days. I saw one earlier today, though I have no memory of it at the moment he's telling me.

An older man, a Maui detective, dressed in casual clothes, approaches me and explains that the search had been called off two hours ago. The forecast predicted that another tropical storm would strike Maui from the northeast tonight with torrential rain, near-freezing temperatures, and gale-force winds that would make the efforts of the search teams dangerous. He explains, in a subdued voice, that each one of the rescue leaders had agreed that I would not be found alive. They also said that if I were still alive before the storm hit tonight, I would not survive it. I nod my head in agreement. I am sure I could not have survived another night, let alone another storm. He finishes by saying that the plan was to resume the search in the first part of the next week in an attempt to recover the body. My body.

Someone hands me a phone and says that my wife is on the line. My first attempt comes out with a rasp. I try again.

"Hi."

"Hi. How are you doing?"

I'm so sorry. I'm really sorry to make you worry.

"I'm glad you're okay."

"I think the ambulance is ready to take me."

"I'll meet you at the hospital."

"Okay. See you then."

"Bye."

The detective looks at me and comments on the shortness of the conversation.

Someone yells out to the search leader, "How did you find him?" The ranger steps up and yells back, her voice full of conviction, "He wasn't found. He walked out on his own."

I see the flashing lights of the ambulance backing toward the fence. Several men climb over the fence and are handed a stretcher. The blankets wrapped around me are taken off, and I'm helped down onto the stretcher and wrapped up again in fresh blankets. I hear talk about getting me over the five-foot-high fence. I hear them struggle, and I feel ashamed of myself. Quickly, I'm handed off to the waiting hands on the other side of the fence, and then they carry me to the ambulance and place me on a gurney. I hear clapping and cheering behind me.

The two EMTs lift and slide the gurney into the ambulance and then fasten it to one side. Tom introduces himself with a smile and asks, "What's your name, sir." I tell him, though it is struggle to speak through the fat wad in my mouth that aches terribly again. He unwraps me from the blankets and sets them aside. I'm shaking with cold. "Don't worry, Rick, we'll get you warm in just a minute." I smile.

With effort, Tom pulls off the mud-encrusted boots and sopping socks and sets them aside without comment. His scissors cut my T-shirt in half, and he lifts me slightly to take it off. Similarly, he cuts off my filthy pants and underwear. I'm embarrassed. I apologize, "I'm so sorry for the mess, for my pants. I had to pee in them so many times. I just got so tired. I couldn't . . . I'm really so sorry."

He smiles gently, "Rick, no problem. Don't be embarrassed. I'll get them off in a jiffy, and then we'll get you warmed up." I try to smile back, but my tongue won't allow for much of one. After he cuts off my underwear, he places several hot packs along my sides and next to my feet. Then he wraps me in fresh-smelling blankets. While the warm comfort relaxes me, it also lets in fear. While he prepares an IV, I say, "I don't know what's wrong with my mouth."

He asks me to open my mouth, and after taking a look says, "Well, your tongue is pretty swollen. Maybe you bit it. Don't worry. The docs will fix you up."

Tom notices that I'm shivering again, "Hey, Rick, I'll get you warmed up." He pulls back the blankets, takes away the depleted heat packs, and lays hot new ones around me. This whole time I keep my eyes closed. The one heat pack under my neck feels good, but I continue shaking. It scares me. I ask, "Am I going to be, okay?"

He turns and looks at me and with an assuring smile, "You're going to be fine, Rick. We'll take good care of you. You're safe now."

CHAPTER 14

RECOVERY

MY arrival at the hospital brings me some clarity until I'm given meds. My wife meets me at the Emergency Room door.

"How are you doing?"

"I'm okay."

"I am glad. I was scared, you dork."

"I know. I am so very sorry for what I put you through."

An examination revealed that my skin was permeated with sand and dirt that had to be removed to prevent infection. It was an excruciating process that involved tubs of hot water, towels, and a scrub brush and which caused me to cry out in pain.

At the hospital, I had an unexpected visit from the detective with Maui police, who questioned me about what happened. I pieced together the events as I remembered them. He asked if I recalled seeing two young couples near Sliding Sands trail, and I replied that I did. He had talked to them, and they had remarked that I was dressed and acting strangely, jogging past them with my head down and saying something about "doing some gardening." I explained that I was in a hurry because I had a late start and didn't want to strike up a conversation. Kimberly had told him that I had a history of depression, He asked me if I was depressed that day, and if I went to the crater to end my life. He wondered if I was ill-prepared and dressed as I was for that reason. I was upset and very angry by his question. It was crazy of him to ask such a thing because the entire time I was lost, I struggled desperately to stay alive.

I told the detective that my lack of preparation was due, ironically, to my extensive outdoor experience. For more than fifty years, I have been climbing mountains. I was embarrassed to explain to him that on the day of the hike I had started off late, the weather was iffy, and I wasn't fully equipped. In the past, I'd always worn appropriate clothes and carried essential items, as well as extra food food, clothing, and emergency gear. But over the years, since I no longer climb anything difficult, or hike for more than a day or two in the backcountry, I have gradually and unthinkingly lightened my load from most of the gear I used to carry. I didn't replenish first-aid supplies and emergency items because I didn't think I would need them. My pack got smaller and lighter. I was lulled into complacency because I never encountered problems. I continue to hike, but I'm significantly better prepared. The pack I carry is larger and bulges with first aid, survival gear, extra food, and clothing. My boots are heavier and waterproof, as is my jacket.

Later in the day, Ranger Conner called me. I am so glad to hear her voice that my words tumble out in disarray. Her care and compassion touched me deeply in those first moments at the Hosmer Grove Campground. She said that she was trying to figure out where I fell under the Park boundary fence and was lost in the rainforest. She wondered if I could remember any of the details. I tell her that I'm sure I will remember all of it. I could write it all up and send it to her. When I hung up I asked my wife if she would write down what I could tell her about what happened— those pages are the foundation for this memoir.

The next morning, the doctor discharged me, saying he didn't know how I managed to survive. From the chart, he read a list of my injuries which included extensive cuts and abrasions over all the exposed parts of the body, including a large contusion on the forehead; tongue puncture by the teeth; significant edema; dehydration; cracked lips and mucous membranes; rhabdomyolysis causing significant muscle pain and potential damage to the heart and kidneys.

On the one hand, as wonderful as it felt to be back home and to talk on the phone to my daughters and friends, on the other hand, it was a very difficult time. I couldn't find a position that didn't cause exhausting pain and had problems eating due to the injury to my tongue. Although I was fussy and irritable, my wife tended to me patiently and without complaint, changing my bandages, administering medications, shopping for my needs, and so much more. My swollen tongue still throbbed, and a dentist verified that two teeth went through the side of my tongue in one of the falls and that there was no treatment except time. Difficult as those days were, they provided an opportunity for me to express my love for the people I cared for and to feel their love for me.

While I recovered, I was absorbed in the task of typing up the notes about my adventure and soon sent them off to Ranger Conners. I didn't remember what she looked like but could still feel the caring power of her kneeling beside me, holding me, making me feel safe. When I called to ask if she'd received the notes, she said she had and wondered if I felt up to revisiting the Park with her to figure out where I had gone. I was eager to do so.

She was waiting for Kimberly and me at the Halemau'u parking lot with maps spread across the hood of her police car. The three of us bent over them, scrutinizing the steep bare slopes of Haleakala outside the crater. From my written description she had a pretty good idea of where I fell under the boundary fence. She placed her finger on the map where we were and made a line with her finger down past a green water tower to a ravine that ran under the fence. Then we look up to see the water tower and the nearby fence with a deep ravine underneath it. I felt strongly that this was the place fell out of the Park and into the Waikamoi Preserve. The

Waikamoi is a refuge for endangered plants and animals. I had never heard of it. Once a month, by reservation only, a group of twelve people led by a guide is allowed to walk several trails through parts of this area. It's a smaller section of a large forest that runs down to the ocean. She had hiked in the Preserve, but she had never been under the fence, into the ravine, and then out into where I had wandered. Maybe no one had except me.

She asked if we would like to walk a mile or so on the Halamau'u trail, the trail I had tried to get up when I turned the corner out of the crater and slammed headlong into the storm. "Yes, I would," I wanted find the various places I went at first: the fence I moved along to avoid the danger of the rim, where I threw off the sweatshirt, and the tree I sat under when the moon came out. After walking a short way down the boulder-strewn trail, I realized I wasn't wearing trail shoes. I'd left them at home. How could I be such an idiot? I was wearing 'slippahs,' pidgin for flip-flops. I was mortified by my mistake and cringed at the fact that Ranger Connors would realize that I really was quite incompetent. She just shrugged it off and said it shouldn't be a problem. I wished I had boots when I got off the trail a few times to wander into the bush to look for the sweatshirt I had peeled off and thrown away. I couldn't find it, but stumbled across the tree where I saw town lights shimmer for a few moments the first night.

Heading back up to the cars, the ranger suggested we drive down to the Hosmer Grove Campground where my journey had ended. I was both very excited and fearful. On the short drive down to Hosmer Grove, I remembered the last hour coming to the campground, the worn out sign I couldn't read, the young girl sitting in the grass, the people gathered around me, and my indescribable weariness and relief.

We got to where the Volkswagen camper had been parked and where I stood at the boundary fence and called for help. We walked down the fence line a short way to the gate—it was much closer than it had seemed that first time. She unlocked the gate, and we looked around into the forest, catching sight of the path. She asked if we'd like to walk up a way, which I did. The trail was steep, and soon we were all a little breathless. We stopped now and then to look around. Kimberly didn't want to go any farther, and I asked the ranger if I could go up a short way while they headed back down. She agreed, but with a warning, which wasn't necessary because I was quite sure of being very careful. I was curious and a bit frightened. The trail continued its steep rise. In a half hour, I notice a barbed wire lying on the ground. Nearby was the sign I couldn't read when I stood there weeks earlier. It was a new sign that I could read: "The Nature Conservancy of Hawaii: Waikamoi Preserve."

I wanted to keep going past the sign, up to that pine-wooded place with the numbered trees. But now looking up into the towering canopy of trees, I knew how easy it would be to get lost again. I turned around and headed back down. A few weeks ago, it had been a dizzying, breathless struggle to climb up this trail. I stopped many times. The fact is, the trail didn't go up at a steep angle at all, but down. I had been so disoriented that while I thought I was struggling to climb up, it was actually an easy walk down. When I got back to my wife and the ranger, I told them about how utterly confused I had been. It was example of the many times I had been delusional.

After that time with Ranger Connor, I wanted to go back to Haleakala alone. As my body healed, the urge became stronger to see where I had gone after I fell under the fence and to follow the small creek to the wall of rock, the pool, and the other places. The morning I returned, the sky was a deep blue, and the slopes up Haleakala's sides were warm and inviting. I parked near Hosmer Grove and made my way up the service trail that goes near the green water tank and the fence where I left the Park. I estimated it would take me about thirty minutes to reach a place where I could leave the trail and bushwhack to the water tank and the fence beyond.

When I left the trail to go toward the tank and on to the fence, the ground was covered with ankle high brush and shallow ravines. I couldn't see the tank or the fence, but I did see the line of trees that marked the end of the Park, and the beginning of the rainforest. The ground got rougher with steeper rises and dips. It was farther than I estimated. At one point, I stumbled against a rock and slipped into a narrow crevice. It was only a foot or two deep, but my heart beat fast with the memories of other falls. How did I ever make it across here through the downpour and pitch-black night? When I got up and started again, I saw the tank and right behind it, the fence. When I reached the fence, I grabbed hold of it, this time wearing leather gloves.

The fence was suspended at least 30-yards and anchored on the other side of the deep ravine. Gripping the top wire, I took a few steps down to where my feet were almost off the ground, then sat with my legs over the edge, looking down to where I had fallen hard against the steep, muddy hill. Now it was dry and not a far drop.

Something caught my eye, a small, yellow object. My baseball cap. Excited to find evidence that I had been here, I want to retrieve it and wear it again. But I didn't know if I would be able to get back up if I went down. The slope was steep but dry, and my desire was strong. Holding on to the bottom strand of wire, I let myself down and touched the ground with my boots digging into the soft dirt. My hat was an arm's length from me. Though covered with mud and wrinkled by the rain, it too, was dry. I put it on my head with a kind of wonder. I couldn't believe I found it.

I stepped carefully along the side of the hill and then down to the edge of this first little pool. It was a lovely place with marsh grass along the banks of the pool, a cliff above it, a stand of immense trees, and the small brook that I walked through toward a much larger pool of water. How opposite from what I experienced before. The tiny stream underfoot was only a few inches deep here, and not more than a foot as I moved on. It all felt so familiar, yet completely different. Ahead, the stream disappeared beneath some boulders. Carefully, I looked down the short cliff and the water below me. This is the place where I slipped off the top boulder and fell into that cold pool.

Stepping off the boulder, I walked over to a grassy place alongside the wall leading to the pool. Halfway down, I saw the crevice that I had fallen into, where my ankle got stuck, the water bottle fell out of its loop, and I banged down the rest of the way into the water. The drop was thirty feet. In the shivering dark, it felt much higher. The fall could have easily knocked me out and caused me to drown.

After skirting the rest of the way down and around the cliff, I walked to the far side of the pool. The sun shone on the fine sand around me. I looked across the pond at the cliff when my eye caught something bobbing in the water. Floating on the surface was my water bottle. With a long branch, I was able to snag it. Although dented and scratched from the fall, it was still half-full of water that would have been great help to me.

The place I stood was like a small beach. Where I stood the pond was shallow then it dropped off slowly, but the night I fell down the wall and plunged into the pool, I found no shallows, but waded in cold water up to my chest. On my right, the mantle shelf is flat and bare above the water where I fought with all my failing strength to get out. Now I can see how easy it would have been to crawl out of the shallow water where I was now standing in the daylight.

For a long time, I sat on the sand with my legs crossed, looking at the wall, the water, the glimmering ferns, and tall trees with a light breeze through them. Flying insects buzzed in the stillness. Birdsong together with the odor of green growing things soothed me. I lay back with my hands clasped behind my head, put the white end of a blade of grass between my teeth, and slowly gazed around me in wonder. I prayed out loud in words of thanksgiving to be alive, and to be here taking in all of this beauty and peace. I marvel at this place of warm safety that had filled me with overwhelming fear. Behind me was the dead tree trunk bleached white. I had walked alongside it in the dark and then left it and crawled up the first of many muddy hills toward what I thought were giants.

I wanted to climb up there again. There was still so much to figure out. Maybe I could find the wire between the trees with the fluttering red ribbon above it, or the boulder-strewn hill on the other side. But a wave of dread washed over me, and I turned back to the small sandy beach, the pool, and the rock wall with green moss in its cracks. I walked back up the grass alongside the rock wall, and sloshed my way in the brook to the first pool of water, up the hillside, and under the fence. I pulled the brim of my yellow baseball cap down to shade my eyes from the sunset, clutched the water bottle to my chest, and walked back to where the car was parked.

EPILOGUE

WHEN people ask me how I survived, I typically respond, "Barely." Sometimes they want to know the impact on me. What it is different about my life now than before the ordeal? Have I made resolutions? Have I found a new direction for my life? Did these experiences bring me closer to God? I've thought long and hard about these questions. I know I have a strong feeling for the preciousness of life. The gift of my family's closeness and unfailing love, and the kindness of friends will bless me all the days of my life. I have felt close to God. I still do. I don't think that this ordeal made significant changes in me. Perhaps, the impact of it all has been felt rather than thought. My survival is inexplicable. I am grateful beyond words.

There were moments in the nights of cold and rain, days of heat, and hours of pain, fear, and desperation that I cried out for help, and then made a decision. I am drawn to the mystery of prayer. When I was sure that I was dying, I knew peace, the peace of letting go. Perhaps, in some way, letting go is the essence of faith.

The local media covered my disappearance, the search, dire predictions, and a happy ending. In the local newspaper, some readers expressed concern and support; others were harsh and critical. One wrote, "What kind of an old fool goes down into that crater by himself anyway?" and another echoed with, "A 62-year-old man has no business being down there in Haleakala, or any other place like that." Since I was sixty-nine years old at the time, I was an older fool than she thought. While it is true that age factors into the risk of some adventures, I feel that, whether physical or emotional, intellectual or artistic, adventures with even a modicum of risk, enrich each of our lives.

My ability and desire for near-the-edge adventure are over, but not the joy of milder forays through the woods; sitting on the boulders of an easy peak's summit, chomping on a slice of cheese and a hunk of bread. These days, more often than not, I go by myself, but when the opportunity comes along to hook up with a hiking buddy, well then, I smile. Companionship in the wild is a gift I cherish. I have been blessed by many pals.

The joy I experience from a variety of adventures call to mind these words of Thoreau in *Walden*:

> *I went to the woods because I wished to live deliberately, to front the essential facts of life, and to see if I could not learn what it had to teach, and not, when I came to die, discover that I had not lived.*

Photo 1. *Satellite Photo of the Island of Maui. The Haleakala volcano covers approximately 3/4 of the island. It encompasses the larger lower portion in the photo. Haleakala National Park is the small brown area. The rainforest of Haleakala is the green area that runs down to the Pacific Ocean.*

Photo 2. *Mists often float above the trails that descend into the Haleakala Crater. They bring cool refreshment to hikers.*

Photo 3. *Clouds flow up through the Ko'olau Gap. This beautiful sight occurs often. In the background on the left side is where the Halemau'u trail climbs out of the crater through a steep series of switchbacks. It was here that the storm hit full force.*

Photo 4. *This species of Silversword is found only here growing between seven and ten thousand feet in the Haleakala volcano and its environs. It lives in the hot, dry climate for fifty years or much more. It blooms once and then dies. The Silverswords give me an anticipated greeting when I first see them.*

Photo 5. *Here is a rugged section of the Waikamoi. I wandered through many places like this, and then others that were totally opposite with wide-open meadows and lava ridges in the distance.*

Photo 6. *This is another view in the rain forest that reveals the rugged variety of the landscape.*

Photo 7. *This is the place where I stumbled into the Hosmer Grove Campground. The first responders had to climb over the fence and lift me on a stretcher. It took ten of them.*

Photo 8. *Two years later, I went back down into the crater with a Colorado buddy to climb lava mounds. There were no lingering physical or emotional after-effects, but a lot of fun.*

Photo 9. *The adventures continue, but certainly not the dangers of past times. Here I stand beneath Squaretop Mountain in Colorado.*

Photo 10. *My best pal, Ron, and I had just completed a rock climb in Boulder Canyon, Colorado. It began raining on the way down. We asked a watching tourist to take our picture. This was in the early 1960s.*

NOTES FROM THOSE WHO WAITED

The following are unedited emails detailing
the reactions of friends and family.

Daughter Heather

I remember first hearing from Kimberly. I was at the Front Range
School in Denver, and I was working my shift at the coffee shop and
so focused on that, and yet felt divided just emotionally, and in my
thoughts about what was going on. It felt so immense, in between,
like not having information and just waiting. And then I just remember many people around me, my friends at the school, knowing what
happened, and constantly asking questions. And then texting my
husband Brent, and letting him know what was going on. And then
my boys, after they got out of school, letting them know what was
going on. It just felt like time was dragging on while they were
searching for you.

So, I can't remember the time exactly. I feel like it was a Friday
night that the boys and I came over to my sister Stef's house. Stef
was sitting in her closet. I remember her sitting on the floor with her
friend Deb. And I went in there and sat on the floor with them, and
we were all just crying. We were just crying and crying. I think we
were sitting in there because we wanted to protect the kids from our
emotions. We didn't want to scare them.

Cole, my oldest boy, was really affected. I remember him lying on the floor of the landing wrapped up in a blanket, and he was listening to Christian music and had his head covered with a blanket, and saying that he was really scared and really sad.

And I think while we were sitting in the closet crying the biggest thing we kept saying was, "Not Dad. Especially like this." I think that was the disconnect we felt. We knew your proficiency in the mountains, and your ability to kind of gauge unsafe situations, and how much experience you had being in the wilderness. It was so confusing, but then again, there was so little information. Then I remember, getting another call from Kimberly that they had called off the search, and that they were going to resume on Monday with a body search.

And just hearing that, and the finality of that. I can't think of the right words. Kind of almost like a haunting, a body search? I think too of you being our dad, and looking at you as being so self-sufficient. Looking at you as just so strong and invincible, and not having the answers of what happened to you. We trusted you, so much, to get out of situations like this, especially in wilderness. It just kind of left me with this big gaping hole of not knowing what actually happened, and would we ever know. And then so, yeah, just the grieving that ensued. It reminded me of what I would think like Jewish families do when they mourn corporately, as they would do as a community. There was no embarrassment. There was no hiding. We, too, were wailing.

Brent had come from coaching, football. I just fell into his arms. He had to support my weight. I've never grieved like that before. All of us were walking through the house crying, and just shaking our heads. We couldn't believe it. And then I know I had gone downstairs, and Stef was still upstairs. I remember Stef coming to the top of the stairs and just screaming, "He's alive!" 'They just found him!" "He's Alive!" And seriously, I never had a bigger swing from absolute despair to the best thing you could ever hope for.

Kimberly had called. I know she was trying to be with you, and also trying to relate to us. She was so conscientious. Because I knew, she knew the state we were all in, and so wanting to give us information, but she just didn't have much information only that you were alive, and the ambulance was coming.

So, then I can't remember whether you were in the ambulance, or the hospital when we got to hear your voice. And just her thoughtfulness for that too. She knew that we would want to hear your voice. It was quite muffled, from your tongue, from the bite. I don't know how to say this. But we knew it was you.

Yeah, the absolute adrenaline rush. If we had been hooked up to some sort of machine that measured feelings. I don't even know like, from the lowest of the lows to absolute elation. I don't feel like many people get that. They don't get to experience grieving someone's death, and then like literally having it totally turn around. But I think the hardest thing I was left with is, that although we got to have the amazing turnaround that people that people wish for, but don't get to have. I got to feel what it would feel like when we do lose you. So, like it sucks because you will die at some point. We all will. I think that's what lingers for me that I know what it feels like I know what it feels to have your dad's life be over. We probably won't get another "do-over" like this.

Then I think, in the days and weeks following, just getting all the updates about your health, and just not feeling that you were out of the woods yet. Wondering if you would come back to being who we knew you to be, strong and capable. But you've clearly done that, Mr. CrossFit. Okay, that's all.

Daughter Stefany

My memory of you getting lost in the Haleakala region was being up in the mountains. We were staying in Breckenridge as a family, the five of us, and I got a call from Kimberly, kind of late one night probably around 9:00 PM. That would have been the first night She said that you were lost because you hadn't gotten back to your car. I remember being really upset and so, I think, we cut our trip really short and we came home the next day. Heather came over, and Laura came over, and my friend Debby came over and we had a house full of people. But basically, I spent the hours just grieving, and wondering, and being fearful, and not really letting down the hope, because they were still searching for you.

A kind of fast-forward to that last night. I remember getting a call from Kimberly saying they called off the search, and just being devastated. I remember going into the master bedroom closet because there were so many people over, and it was loud. And I just remember as if I could never stop sobbing, I thought, at that point, that you were gone. And the fact that they were calling off the search, I realized there was absolutely no hope. That was it, and we were going to have to say goodbye without any kind of closure.

So, I was in my closet surrounded by my friends. I remember Laura came in the closet with me, one of my friends Debbie. My sister-in-law, Libby, was downstairs. Aunt Dot was down there too. I think it was just like an hour-and-a-half just crying, and being upset, and questioning and wondering why you could not be found. And why they would be calling off the search. And at that stage where you're just angry at the people, the professionals, for what they were doing.

And then I just remember my phone rang, and Kimberly called again and said you had been found. And I think I just came out of the closet and started screaming and running downstairs. And it was just like, literally, it was probably the most extreme joy I had ever experienced in my life. It was a flood of emotion.

I felt tremendous relief, and tremendous joy at the same time. I felt ecstatic. And I just remember screaming and crying, and screaming and crying, and laughing. And then at that point, we all gathered, everyone that was over. I remember Heather, Brent, the boys, Libby, Aunt Dot, Laura, Debra, my kids, and we just kept talking, and trying to repeat what we had heard from Kimberly about you coming into the campsite, and stumbling in, and wondering about your condition.

And the phone rang again, and it was you this time, and your voice was really slurry and thick. But you were like, "Hi pal. I'm okay." And I think you also probably talked to Heather or I had you on speaker at that point so everybody could hear you. And we were so grateful. And I remember Aunt Dot, before we found out they had called off the search she asked if we could pray for you. Then later, when we found out you were found or came to be found, she said we need to thank God for Rick being safe. And she cried too, really hard.

Well, yeah, that's what I remember, just the dramatic, overwhelming sense of relief, and something that felt so impossible, and so dark, that we'd just have to go on and grieve, and that you were dead, and that's just all there was, and no closure. And then to have it turn around was amazing.

Later I remember going through my emails. And I had a folder named, "Dad's writing." And I just remembered I had that from you. That I could hold on to in your absence. Occasionally, I have dreams that you are gone, that you are lost. I do have these dreams of reliving the situation because it was traumatic.

Daughter Shannon

Come home

"Have they found Papa yet?"

Bobo asks. Yet…it means he will, right?

My dad is missing.

I vacillate between complete grief and a disbelief dream.

How is this possible.

The call came this morning.

He was hiking in Maui, supposed to return last night, and did not come home.

Deveraux said she was supposed to go climbing rocks with Papa…

She loves to climb, and I had told her, papa and she would go.

She said if he doesn't get here, they will climb rocks in heaven.

I don't want them to climb rocks in heaven, not yet.

In the midst of the day, Deveraux, my 8-year-old, gives me this note:

"Dear Mama, I know how scared it feels to be missing your dada and then he is missing sometimes. I ask a lot of questions when I am sad. Jesus is with him."

Love, Deveraux

We are all waiting.

Where is he?

Where are you, Dad?

This is not supposed to be…

We are not ready

My mother-in-law called me, she said, "He is going to be okay." How did she know this?

I just want to talk to him. I just want to hear his voice. I just want to pick up the phone and just touch base. I did call his cell phone to tell him I love him, to tell him I am sorry I haven't emailed him recently. I feel so guilty about that. And yet, I know he knew.

Deveraux said, "It is not a normal day without Papa."

I just keep praying,

He loved Earthbound farm...close to where we live in California.

He loved reading this blog.

My friend watched my kids so I can watch the ocean and pray.

I pray, "Come home dad" It is all I can pray. "Come home."

Friday, September 27

They are calling off the search for our dad.

The weather is not good.

They will not search until Monday.

They are not hopeful.

I could hardly breathe

Heather called me outside Safeway.

There is this funny thing in the midst of tragedy, when you don't know the outcome, sometimes you keep moving. I kept moving. We were hosting our farewell gathering at the beach in a couple of days and in gathering supplies, I felt the need to keep moving forward.

So, in the middle of the Safeway parking lot, there I was with the most devastating news.

"No, no, no, no!"

This can't be.

I am pushing my cart down the parking lot, the loud clatter matching the craziness I feel.

I am gasping.

It is guttural.

Real and still not.

I just want one more

One more talk. Just one more.

There is no one who loves me the way my dad does…. on his way to his Shanny

The van with my family waiting inside picks me up. I don't know how to do this.

Andrew and I, thankfully, have a place for our kiddos for the evening. It is just him and I, and we go to the water's edge. Always a comfort.

It hit me there that night, as we watched the ocean, This is the hope of glory.

Dad, if you are off that mountain and so with Jesus, we will see you.

The hope of glory. This is not a positive spin.

This is the only hope we have this side of heaven.

Dad, I love you so much.

I want to talk to you about all of this.

I groan. It is real. It is a dream.

I just want one more time.

Andrew and I walk the streets of Carmel by the Sea. Numbing believing disbelief.

Friday, September 27… later that evening.

The first thing I notice is the light in the completely dark house. I will never forget that lamp. When we left the house, it was light outside. Now coming back to the darkness, the only light was that battery-operated candle that shone.

We went inside and looked at plane tickets. We wanted Andrew to go and help look, do anything. We were helpless on the other side of the ocean.

The phone rang. It was Kimberly.

She spoke these three words, "HE IS ALIVE!"

I let out a groan, similar to a pregnancy groan.

We went from the utter depths of despair to crazy heights of Joy.

I have never been in that place of grief, then go to that kind of relief. Ever.

I get one more time.

Jesus has answered our prayer.

He has granted mercy.

He heard our groans.

He heard.

thank you for the prayers of belief, my people who were praying.

Saturday, September 28

He came back!

I watched the sun go down tonight on the beach in such a different place as I had watched the sun go down on the water last night. I did not want the sun to go down last night. It just felt like something would be final. Just last night, the world had turned upside down.

I talked to dad tonight. I waited all day. It was so good to hear his voice. He is not fully himself, of course. Tired, sore throat…. alive! It was his voice to me, Shanny.

It is such a strange thing. To talk to someone, you thought you never would see again this side of heaven. I imagined telling him I love him and getting that one more time. I groaned for that. It happened. I got to tell him I love him and hear him say it back.

It feels like he came back to life. In my heart, I was feeling the loss of him. He came back to life!

Enlarge and increase my faith. God, you listen, act on our behalf, you are affected by us and just love us so much.

He answered.

Yell it from the mountaintop, "He is alive!!!"

A year later, we had the privilege of walking the places that almost took dad from us. We were honored to hear the story of a tale that could have had a very different ending. We could barely picture him being out there alone, and lost now as the three of us in the daylight were out for a hike.

It was staggering to realize how perspective is everything.

He has so turned around and in such a different spot on the mountain than he thought he was… but it is hard to see in the dark. How glad we are for our ending.

Hosmer's Grove now is a sacred space. It always will be. The birds were so loud this summer after a pandemic quieted the crowds, which only made the space more sacred.

This is one of my faith stories. It is a reference point for answered prayer.

My prayer. My dad's prayer.

"The Lord heard my cry, and he answered." He brought him home.

Son-in-Law Roy

First, I was shocked that they couldn't find you. I was appalled by the lack of organization and concerted effort to put a search team together. It seemed willy-nilly enough that I was going to fly to Maui myself to help organize a volunteer grid search. I used to do people searches in the foothills of Boulder with the Boulder County rescue squad. I was planning on getting my tickets that evening when Kimberly had called, stating that they were stopping the search. Then I was so relieved when we got the call that you had found your way back.

Good old Aunt Dot was the first to remind us to pray—offering a simple childlike prayer for your deliverance and also stopped all our celebration to give a prayer of thanksgiving.

Best Friend Ron, "Got my Pal Back."

Two old men who have been friends since the first hairs grew on their skinny legs have clearly figured out how to get along when things get rough. Picture a couple of puppies in fresh snow, chasing, yapping, sniping at each other, rolling down a hill, falling off an icy log, gamboling. And then one of the puppies runs into the highway, freezes in front of a bus, then crouches as the iron beast passes over. Passed over. That might sum it up for me that day when I learned my pal somehow crawled into a campground barely alive. He did what? On a dead volcano? In Hawaii? Ill-prepared? Nearly froze? We've been on a few mountains in Colorado. We've roped up, nailed spikes into rocks, hooked rings to them, pulled ourselves up and up, cleaned away the "aid" properly so the next climbers would find nothing, and eased down ropes to end beautiful days in our Rockies, our home sweet home. And once when I slipped, he was prepared, tied into the rock above me, slowed the zipping rope, broke my fall, lowered me to a ledge, descended himself, then nursed us both to terra firma. And a dead volcano in Hawaii almost brought him down? No way. Yes, way. His wife contacted me, and told me what had happened, the frightening details laid out. Stories in the newspapers. Helicopter searches, dogs, witnesses. Of course, I read all that several times, telephone calls to Hawaii, then the hospital stay, the near failure of vital organs. My puppy pal nearly died. But… he didn't. You want to know what it's like to almost lose your pal, of course, you do. Here's what it's like—like nothing else. Don't want to think about it, don't want to talk about it, don't want to recount the thoughts, the emotions. Don't want that because here's what it's like now. We're still meeting for cocktails. He's still helping me figure out the meaning of everything. We still hug and smile. He bounds up Colorado mountains, goes to his exercise class, and leaves me mostly in the dust, or waiting in the car. Doesn't matter, because we're pals still able to be together. We're pals, and I still got him, and the dead volcano doesn't. That's life, friends. That's friends, life. Got my pal. Still. Still got my pal.

ROUTE DURING THE FIRST HOURS

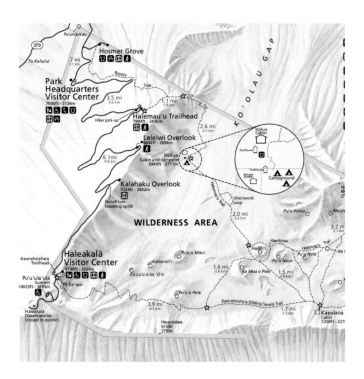

Photo 11. *Trail map of the rim and inside of the crater marking important places in the story.*

THE summit of Haleakala rises to ten thousand feet, and the descent on the Sliding Sands trail to the Kapalaoa cabin at the crater is 2,773 at a distance of approximately four and a half miles from the top. The trail continues from there to the Paliku cabin just over two miles from Kapalaoa near the end of the crater. The crater runs approximately seven miles long by two miles wide. It is silent, without a breath of wind. There is no bird song, mosquito buzz, or running water. Just before I arrived at the cabin was the place where the two young couples sat on either side of the trail and questioned my words and appearance.

At the Kapalaoa cabin, I rested a few minutes, and then turned on to one of three sketchy trails that cross the crater here. It meanders between the Pu'u Nole and Pu'u Naue cinder cones where after a mile the trail ends at the Halemau'u trail. A left turn on the Halemau'u leads to the Holua cabin about three miles away. A right turn on the same path leads to a steep climb up the switchbacks that come out of the crater where my old Corolla would be waiting for me at the parking lot. Of course, I never arrived at the parking because a few steps around that corner, I was blasted by the torrent and lost my way.

GLOSSARY

Alpenglow — a reddish glow seen near sunset or sunrise on the walls and summit of a mountain.

Carabiner — a usually D-shaped aluminum or steel link of various shapes used by rock climbers as a connection with rope or sling.

Couloir — a steep narrow gully on a mountainside.

Delusion — a false belief.

Flatirons — steep and tilted sandstone rock formations in Boulder, Colorado.

Glissading — sliding down steep snow or ice often with an ice ax for safety.

Haleakala National Park — designated a national park in 1961 to protect the native Hawaiian ecosystem and provide recreation opportunities for visitors.

Haleakala Observatories — an observation site located near the summit of a tropical inversion layer that provides excellent viewing for astrophysical research.

Halemau'u Trailhead — it begins as a steep, narrow descent to the floor of the crater and to the Holua cabin, then turns to cross the crater.

Hallucinations — perception without an external stimulus and with a compelling sense of their reality.

Holua Cabin — located at 6,940 feet nestled at the base of the crater wall near the switchbacks on the Halemau'u where, at the top, I hit the storm head-on.

Hanawi Natural Area Reserve — a large protected area on the wet slopes of the north flank of Haleakala where part of the journey may have taken place.

Hina — Hina is a goddess in many Polynesian and Hawaiian legends. In this myth, she is the mother of Maui.

Hosmer Grove Campground — the only drive-in campground in Haleakala National Park is located at an altitude of nearly seven thousand feet.

'ill'ahi — a Sandalwood tree

Kahului — the town adjacent to Wailuku in north-central Maui with an airport and major industrial and shopping areas.

Kapalaoa Cabin — located along the Sliding Sands Trail at 7, 250-feet, where I turned to catch the Haleamau'u Trail between the cinder cones.

La — the sun god in of myth of Haleakala.

Maui — A demigod, Maui is the great hero and a trickster in the history of many of the Polynesian island cultures as well as Hawaii. His origins vary from culture to culture, but many of his main exploits are similar.

Nene — a species of endangered goose endemic to the Hawaiian Islands and its state bird.

Pele — goddess of fire.

Pitch — the length of a technical climb that can be protected by one rope length.

Piton — a metal spike of various sizes and shapes driven into a crack to support a climber or rope.

Pueo — the Hawaiian, short-eared owl, endangered and found nowhere else in the world. A subspecies of the American short-eared owl.

Pu'u Naue — A red-gray cinder cone on the floor of the Haleakala crater.

Pu'u Nole — A cinder cone adjacent to Pu-Naue. A trail from Sliding Sands Trail connects with the Halemau'u Trail near my crossing to Halemau'u.

Rappel — The act of descending a mountain or cliff on a rope that is attached above.

Rhabdomyolysis — damaged muscle tissue releases its proteins and electrolytes into the bloodstream. These substances can damage the heart and kidneys.

Sling (climbing) — a section of nylon webbing sewn together in a loop for a variety of technical rope climbing purposes.

Silversword — the unique plant lives up to ninety years, flowering only once, sending up a stock of silver hairs.

Sliding Sands Trail — Sliding Sands Trail begins at an altitude of ten thousand feet and descends to the crater floor.

Supply Trail — a trail that climbs from near the Haleakala National Park entrance one thousand feet to intersect the Haleamau'u trail.

Waikamoi Preserve — the Preserve protects hundreds of native birds and plants.

Wailuku — the county seat of Maui County with 17,700 residents.

Wiliwili — a large dryland tree with colorful flowers that range from light cream to bright orange. In the past, it was the desired wood for surfboards.

ATTRIBUTIONS

Quotations

Henry David Thoreau. *Walden, or, a Life in the Woods.* 1854. www.thoreau-online, public domain.

Mark Twain. *Roughing It.* 1872. https://gutenberg.org/files/3177/ebook/3177, public domain.

Photos

Cover. Shannon Gallagher, public domain.

Photo 1. "Maui Satellite Photograph," ww.usgs.gov/media/images.

Photo 2. "Haleakala Crater Trail," public domain from www.goodfreephotos.com.

Photo 3. "Haleakala Crater Ko'olau Gap,' by James Wheeler licensed under Pexels free use.

Photo 4. "Kapalaoa Cabin," by Starr Environmental licensed under CC BY 2.0.

Photo 4. "Silversword Plant," by Navin75 licensed under CC BY-SA 2.0.

Photo 5. "Waikamoi-Maui," by Starr Environmental licensed under C C BY 2.0.

Photo 6. "Stream-Waikamoi-Maui," by Starr Environment licensed under CCC BY 2.0.

Photo 7. "Hosmer Grove Campground Fence," public domain.

Photo 8. "Rick Climbing in Haleakala Crater," public domain.

Photo 9. "Beneath Square Top Mountain," public domain.

Photo 10. "Rick and Ron," public domain.

Photo 11. "Haleakala National Park Summit Area Short Trail Hike," nps.gov/hale/planourvisit/maps.

ACKNOWLEDGMENTS

Thanks to Ron Stewart and Dvir Abramovich for reading the manuscript and giving me their kind support. Mark Feder provided a flow of creative ideas, helpful direction, and encouragement for which I am grateful.

Alice Longaker is my editor. Her expertise, patience, and wisdom brought this book to fruition. She provided guidance for the technical aspects of the book and the narrative. I am grateful for her partnership in this memoir, and for the many years of abiding friendship.

Finally, to Katherine, who always listened, encouraged, and gave her gentle love.